Also by Marie Ponsot

The Bird Catcher
The Green Dark
Admit Impediment
True Minds

SPRINGING

SPRINGING

New and Selected Poems

by Marie Ponsot

 Alfred A. Knopf   New York   2002

THIS IS A BORZOI BOOK
PUBLISHED BY ALFRED A. KNOPF

www.randomhouse.com/knopf/poetry

Knopf, Borzoi Books, and the colophon are registered trademarks of Random House, Inc.

Some of the poems in this collection were previously published in the following works:
True Minds, copyright © 1956 by Marie Ponsot (City Lights, San Francisco, as number 5 in the Pocket Poets Series, 1956). • *Admit Impediment,* copyright © 1981 by Marie Ponsot (Alfred A. Knopf, New York, 1981). • *The Green Dark,* copyright © 1988 by Marie Ponsot (Alfred A. Knopf, New York, 1988). • *The Bird Catcher,* copyright © 1998 by Marie Ponsot (Alfred A. Knopf, New York, 1998).

Grateful acknowledgment is made to the following publications, in which some of the new and previously uncollected poems originally appeared:
City I: "Ville Indigène" and "Sam Refuted, Respectfully"; *Columbia:* "Quick It Can" and "Crude Cabin, At the Brink of Quiet"; *Commonweal:* "What Would You Like to Be When You Grow Up?" and "Entranced"; *The New Yorker:* "My Word Is My Bond"; *The Paris Review:* "Ghosts of Narrative"; *Penny Poems, New Haven:* "To Forbid Grief"; *Poetry:* "A Visit," "Ritournelle," "Private and Profane," "Anniversary," and "Elegy for Elizabeth Bleecker Averell"; *The Yale Review:* "Antepenultimate" and "The First, At the Last."

"The Crow Dressed in Peacock Feathers" and "A Tale Told by Atheneus" from *Selected Fables and Tales of La Fontaine,* translated by Marie Ponsot (Signet Classics, New American Library, New York, 1966).

Library of Congress Cataloging-in-Publication Data
Ponsot, Marie.
Springing : new and selected poems / by Marie Ponsot.
p.   cm.
ISBN 0-375-41389-8
I. Title.
PS3531.O49 S67 2002
811'.54—dc21   2001038432

Manufactured in the United States of America
First Edition

TO THE MUSE OF DOORWAYS EDGES VERGES

Tall in the doorway stands
the gentle visitor.
I catch my breath

    (She's quite deaf,
    not interested in
    details of my decor.
    Her few words amaze me.
    Her visits are irregular,
    brief. When our eyes meet,
    how I am drawn to her.
    I keep honey cakes, in case,
    in the freezer. Once
    she stayed for tea.)

She smiles. She speaks up, some.
Each word ravishes,
bright with the sciences
she practices
in the music business.

"One day, when you're not dumb,
you must come
to my place," she says,
and vanishes.

Contents

Uncollected Poems, 1946–1971

From *True Minds*, 1956

From *Admit Impediment,* 1981

From *The Green Dark,* 1988

From *The Bird Catcher,* 1998

New Poems

OLD JOKES APPRECIATE

Up the long stairs I run
stumbling, expectant.
Impatience is hopelessly
desperate.   Hope
takes time.

Sort out the private from the personal.
Advance on losses at a decent pace.

"Aside from all that, Mrs. Lincoln,
how did you like the play?"

DRUNK & DISORDERLY, BIG HAIR

Handmaid to Cybele,
she is a Dactyl, a
tangle-haired leap-taking
hot Corybantica.

Torch-light & cymbal-strikes
scamper along with her.
Kniving & shouting, she
heads up her dancing girls'
streaming sorority, glamorous
over the forested slopes of Mt. Ida

  until she hits 60 and
  loses it (since she's supposed
  to be losing it, loses it).
  Someone takes over
  her sickle & signature tune. Soon
  they leave her & she doesn't care.

  Down to the valley floor
  scared she won't make it, she
  slipslides unlit to no rhythm,
  not screaming. But now she can
  hear in the distance
  some new thing, surprising.
  She likes it. She wants it.
  What is it? Its echoes originate
  sober as heartbeats, her beat,
  unexpected. It woos her.

The rhythm's complex
—like the longing to improvise
or, like Aubade inside Lullaby
inside a falling and rising
of planets. A clouding. A clearing.
She listens. It happens
between her own two ears.

ORIGIN

The skull or shell
or wall of bone shaped
with its egg advantages
does not advertise

the gardens it contains,
the marriages, the furies,
or the city it shelters
(clangs, clouds, silences,
found souls crowding,
big dank cans where things
putrify)

or the glade it hides
for us to hide in, where
—our lives eased open—
we drowse by the pond and wake
beside ourselves with thirst,
where (dipping the cup we find)
we get of necessity
a drink of some depth
full of taste
and original
energy.

The darling face,
the fragrant chevelure,
even the beautiful ears

on the shell do not
boast about the workplace inside.

They prefer to appear to agree
they are just along for the ride.

WHAT WOULD YOU LIKE TO BE
WHEN YOU GROW UP?

I

Here I am in the garden
on my knees digging
as if I were innocent,
gloveless in island soil—
     sandy, unstable,
     hardly soil at all,
     very sharp and mineral.

Planted to temper the heat,
this garden has trees & fruit trees.
After a stormy spring
it's a low-walled well of green
bouncing into blossoming.
Already it turns me
toward autumn crocus now in leaf,
chrysanthemum, feverfew,
white & gold after the pears drop.

It's at its best in winter,
free of me, as I imagine it—
its six wonderful places to sit
(next to the tarragon and sage,
under the dogwood for breakfast,
on a log beside the speedwell).

It has taught me
     planning which is essential
          is impossible.

Mistakes (bittersweet, honeysuckle)
come back every year
hugely bountiful. So do
the peonies, lilies, & daylilies,
& grandma's rampant rose.

Dear garden of my making
stuffed with my ideas & sweat,
you are reasonable.
Your pleasure
is, like me, physical.

So, behave.
I can't keep counting on my fingers
to make sure all your parts are on hand.

I head for the kitchen, to cook.
I have no other plans.

You were not what I needed after all.

2

The reason for the garden is
this rooming house, this tidy
body's heart, my minded body

where I now rent only
the attic regularly,
and the kitchen, on odd nights.

It is the shabby residence
or sidereal repeat
of recurrent astonishment.
And it has known in every room

the othering bliss of child,
my child, each child different
for each other's sake, each
blessing me blind,
tenant & ceaseless & tiresomely
teaching me
relentlessly
to reach joy by choosing
to love. I so choose, I think.

Only the rich can choose to be poor.
There must be something I can do.

I think I've got whatever I need
in the overhead compartment.

NOW THEN

For a moment I know
I know what can be known.
Error abandons me
breathing an air
of blinding candor.

Candid,
        elated between
rivers twisting through stone
I draw close to home
and am not alone
alone.

        Time outlasts the moment.
        Felicity goes thin.
        It loses translucence,
        fades to transparency,
        and faithfully
        its cleared glass makes
        the other side known.

DECORUM, REFLECTION

Horace, decorous,

glimmers reflected
watching her gestures, in
brazier-lit glimpses
over her shoulder.

He sees her ivory
(under his urging)
gleam in the opposite
mirrors, her mouth soft,

her eye-lidded eyes
twinned like the nipples
rosy and rising
below her collar-bone.

Pleased he is pleasing,
he is well-meaning.
Subtly admiring,
he knows her by name.

Oiled, warm, they soon turn
in to each other.
Business is business.
No longer chatty,
not quite done laughing,
lithe young Lalage
welcomes him home.

GHOSTS OF NARRATIVE

Exodus 4:24–26

I

In the stories that make us
        they wait mysterious
for us to sleep, & wake them
so they can change us,
cruising in currents of feeling
stirred against the tide.

Job's daughters turn up first
in good shoes, alert & able,
saying, "Did you hear that!?
Who does he think he is!"

Lot's daughters look up
and stop crying.

Dinah brushes her torn hair dry.

Deborah honeycombed
by the verdicts of her prophecies
joins them.

When we glimpse them again, each
tells another's story as her own
and then, together,
these fine young women laugh.

2

The Egyptian sprig
who salvaged Moses
from among the rushes
slips past us in profile
usable, useful, used.

Zipporah the Midian,
Moses' next alien life-guard,
strides mum
through the quarreling crowd
        that stumbles hungry
toward the Promised Land.

Moses is left in the lurch
        held back, holding back,
listening to history. There
Sara foresees him, Moses.
He is the mother of his people (us)

Mr. Elsewhere, hill-topped,
held, holding promise.
Sara grieves for him,

till she observes
how well off he is,
        is the only one to get there,
        is the Promised Land,
fertile and
extraterritorial,
        is, under his tongue, at ease

as an answer for her, Sara
our promiser.

Her avoidance of angels
is effortless.
She calls Isaac to her.
"A promise," she says, "is
a promise," and they laugh.

METAPHYSICA

1.   *"Off the Rack," said Wittgenstein to Descartes*
What I'm in is a predicament
of course, and its course
is coarse, even in my eyes.

It's ill-cut, but fitting,
eccentric, ridiculous,
and just my size.

2.   *"The Subject is the Object," said Wittgenstein to Freud*
The subject
rejected as suspect
objects to objects.

The object
rejected as abject
objects.

3.   *What He Said to His Friends*
I long to be
just
in time.

4.   *What He Said to Me*
If I'm not in the forest to see them
do the leaves of my forest glisten?

I cannot ask you to listen to
me unless you listen.

5.   *What He Really Said*
I decline
to decline.

QUICK IT CAN

Quick quick nothing
is broken, sweep up the mess,
bag it, twist it shut,
down the disposal chute with it—
a lumpy drop, bump thud
and out of mind, gone.

Turn the music up a little,
lean more on the bass,
get your equipoise back
with the drum-ripple
that your solar plexus
picks up as pleasure.
It'll steady your stride.

Oh and look out the window, over-look,
I mean, the area of this latest disaster—
let it go. Admire
the seagulls' sail, high
up the skyscraper thermals,
their sea cry, that mewl, their purposeful
surveillance of their world.

By the time they locate & grab
their next meal, the sack of bad writing
—bad, dim-witted, self-serving, sloppy, bad—
will be baled for dumping.
Don't worry. It won't come back to haunt you.
Change your pencil or try pen or

boot up some old stuff you still like
and work on that, if you can find any,
and I think you can; if it can't come back
to haunt you, though I think it can.

RODS & CONES, & THE STATUTE OF LIMITATIONS

"It's the averted eye
that catches sight of leopards
slipping through the midnight hedges
toward the house. Cones track
a stab of flashlight, but it's rods
whose illiterate vision of the night
grabs the shadows & explains
what's that beside me or what
glides up silent on me from behind—
rods, and wits. Yes
wits, as in, 'I had a feeling.'

I had a feeling you'd call.
I caught a glimpse of someone
in the rush coming out of the subway
and I thought, 'It's time. It's you.'

I was empty when we met, back then.
I know I owe you everything—Kafka, Mary Butts, *The Idea
of the Holy,*
the way to wear scarves,
        to welcome brutal losses,
a talent for courteous silences.
I owe it all to you. A huge debt.

But I'm not frightened.
The doorbell's broken, the doorman
doesn't know you, the phone's off the hook,

the E-mail's unplugged,
I live on a very high floor,
and I've been sound asleep for hours."

WHAT CHANGES

1

Pliny's Encyclopedia says: Look
at all the window boxes, greening
on the skimpy sills of the city's poor—
Venus-altars! kept to speak
their longing
for the lost the country past,
their lost haven in the
springing world, their pastoral.

Put the bull to the ready cow.
put the seed in the warming soil:
farm work makes time for farmers;
farm work makes sense to them.

Necessity herself once housed in them
pitiless   and domestic
        as the ram or cat.
Only a growing longing is left to them.

2

Born urban, I locate the lost
where I last saw it, stuck stark
somewhere in a closet, shelved.

Morning sun smacks down
on the wind-hit greens
of my Noho terrace.

The beans survive by toughening
too tough to eat. Lilies stay short
affording just one flower to a stalk.
Plants so stressed live
feebly or freakily, even
the hardest to garden—
like the moonflowers, two months early
in their distress
blossoming a dozen a night
in their rush toward seed.
Their big petals
rip in the crosswinds but
their big fragrance circulates
attractively echoing
responsive life

lost to me, shrunk in my century
to the stutter of occasional balconies
or charming second houses
for Sunday-sized refreshment.

Vergil, Horace, Pliny, Theocritus
you didn't know the half of it.
Only the longing has grown.

3

I reach far back
to my grandmother's neighbor
grounding a boy desperately restless
        with a broken ankle,
keeping him busy like her,
telling him stories of soon,

handing him pails of seeds
to be sorted for next year's planting
within her sweet alyssum borders.

END OF OCTOBER

Leaves wait as the reversal of wind
comes to a stop. The stopped woods
are seized of quiet; waiting for rain
bird & bug conversations stutter to a
stop.
Between the road
and the car in the road and me in the car,
and the woods
and the forms standing tall and the broken
forms and the small forms that crawl there,
the rain begins to fall. Rain-strands,
thin slips of vertical rivers, roll
the shredded waters out of the cloud
and dump them puddling to the ground.
Like sticks half-drowned the trees
lean so my eyes snap some into
lightning shapes, bent & bent.
I leave the car to see where, lower,
the leaves of the shrubs beaten goldleaf
huddle together. In some spaces
nothing but rain appears.

Whatever crosses over
through the wall of rain
changes; old leaves are
now gold. The wall is
continuous, doorless. True,
to get past this wall

there's no need for a door
since it closes around me
as I go through.

ENTRANCED

1

For openers
any wall has doors in it.

Openers who want
a door (not for air
but for passing through)

open & shut it
forcefully, under
heavy pressure
from the atmosphere
outside.

The ideal opener investigates
those osmotic waterfalls
which infiltrate
doorless walls.

2

To enter the enclosure
of the garden
or the citadel

be door, be son
or daughter

to the dearness
of pleasure.

Exits are disclosure.
Making an exit
can unlock you—
the way entrances do—

to being
outgoing.

In verse & reverse
word and worm
both turn.

REAL ESTATE:
Kripplebush, New York

Having measured all the edges and seen
the dry-ridge landmarks of the property,
the salesman sells it (whatever that means).
Lawyers search title, convey deeds, decree
(whatever that means) it belongs to me.

I search too. True titles of this place are: Green
(evergreen) and Sky (fluency, canopy).

Low among leaves & needles, winds careen
with rushed sounds of water—and cross the sky
lisping like water changing its ground.

These deeds are unconveyed, and simplify
beyond all measure into moving sound.

I wake to walk here, walk to learn my bounds.

CRUDE CABIN, AT THE BRINK OF QUIET

An hour after the reminder
of a late September rain,

the cascade of water from the gutter
under the rippled tin roof into the water barrel

is over. Slackening to dripping
it's arriving at stillicide.

Planctum. Punctum.
Silences
      gradually
(drop) to next (drop)
lengthen,
      slowing

like the breath of falling
through thought toward sleep

like the pulse of the blood
between amorous play and dressing

like the pulse of pain
from sharp to sore during healing,

each drop's a signal event,
punctual, rendering a curve
declining as it turns

into silence that turns
into sound that, spent,
turns into silence again.

OUT OF WATER

A new embroidery of flowers, canary color,
       dots the grass already dotty
       with aster-white and clover.

I warn, "They won't last, out of water."
The children pick some anyway.

In or out of water
children don't last either.

I watch them as they pick.
Still free of what's next
       and what was yesterday
they pick today.

PATHETIC FALLACIES ARE BAD SCIENCE BUT

(on reading Susanne K. Langer's *Mind*)

If leaf-trash chokes the stream-bed,
reach for rock-bottom as you rake
the muck out. Let it slump dank,
and dry fading, flat above the bank.
Stand back. Watch the water vault ahead.
Its thrust sweeps the surface clean, shores the debris,
as it debrides its stone path to the lake,
clarity carrying clarity.

To see clear, resist the drag of images.
Take nature as it is, not Dame nor Kind.
Act in events; touch what you name. Abhor
easy obverts of natural metaphor.
Let human speech breathe out its best poor bridges
from mind to world, mind to self, mind to mind.

Yet, I admit the event of the wood thrush:
In a footnote Langer (her book rapids-clean
like the spring-water aired over sleeked rock)
says she witnessed an August bird in shock
when a hawk snatched its mate. It perched, rushed
notes fluting two life-quotas in one flood,
its lungs pushing its voice, flushing the keen
calls, pumped out as the heart pumps blood,

not in twilight or warning but noon & wrong,
its old notes whistled too fast but accurate.

I read this drenched in bird-panic, its spine-
fusing loss all song, all loss; that loss mine
awash in unanswered unanswered song.
And I cannot claim we are not desolate.

ANTEPENULTIMATE

His work describes for us
eons of cycles of sun, drought,
earthquake, ice, calm,
& what they have done for us.
He earns his living learning
history & likelihood
by reading trees, sliced dead ones.
Me too but

with live ones, some of them
aged & hollowing, for instance
this pear tree
                    its elbow extending
one tall young branch
good for a decade or so
leafed out & flexibly
offering for ripening
its always ante-
penultimate pear.

AT THE BOTANICAL GARDENS,
UNIVERSITY OF BRITISH COLUMBIA

The lyf so short, the craft so long to lerne,
th'assay so hard, so sharp the conquering,
the dredful joy, alway that slit so yerne,
all this mene I by Love...

CHAUCER, *Parliament of Fowles*

Among the sepals crisping
where they strain apart to show
tips of blushy petals getting set
to push each other outward
into bloom, the bud
is readying
to extend its destiny.

The parts—the drinking roots
the arching leaves the gorgeous
come-hither blossoming,
the dredful joy in days of time—
maintain their efforts separately

though the loft & drift
of heavy odor from the heart
as petals open over it
proclaim their joyful unity
even as it dissipates.

AFTER-IMAGE, CORTES ISLAND

1

Decorated, and visible
by the blur of white
on its blackish package,
the bald-headed eagle is roosting

forty feet up,
hugging the blackish trunk
of the kingly fir tree,

sixty feet tall & still growing
in a straight thrust, its down-sloped
feathery branches pliant,
accommodating sweeps of wind by
lifting, sinking, lifting.

2

For a few days in summer
we live among eagles
                    casually
above a bouldered shore
among & under the Douglas firs.

Early sun races
to reflect along the water
a blinding stroke
that it shoots out

aimed here.
We must blink at it.

Eyes shut, the after-image
lasts in a retinal blaze.
It persists, pulsing
its edges poignant,
its colors changing
          chameleon lightning
          as its image goes into
          reversal, a swelling
          gold-edged diminishing

and after a couple of minutes
is gone like
remembering
unwillingly.

MY WORD IS MY BOND

"The neighborhood's older now
but it's still
a valley between vaults of stone.
Your corner grocery's gone.

When I walk there I've never left there.

I haunt the place
  where my honor died.

I keep
     a watching
         brief.

When you said
     Now do you love me?
I picked up my ripped shirt
and lied."

WE STAND OUR GROUND

As the earth comes to light,
so the mind to metaphor.

Remotely, they meet, those carriers.
Though either one be more, or less,
or nothing, current spurts
from thrown switch through socket
as they operate.

Wiry between them, and live,
I say my *I* and claim
the chemistry to speak
when words thrill & drive

—uncertainly, certainly—

fusing, taking liberty
evoking a reality that only
syntactic links guarantee.

As hands are to earth,
as eyes are to mind,
so is mind to memory.

STRONG, OFF ROUTE 209

Armstrong
is blowing the roof off
over the coffee-stop's
back-of-the-counter
radio.

She puts down her coffee
and rides with him;
the old woman wings with him
out, into her upper airs.

When he starts to sing
she shuts her eyes
and mouths the words
right on time
delicious

Louis Armstrong, summa
cum laude, young Lester
Young's young University.

IMAGINE THAT

May morning, and the child
in ironed overalls squats
to report to herself
on the poise of a silk-smooth
stone. She hefts it
in her right hand, shifts it
to her left, inspects,
strokes, tries a quick lick,

and sets it down, almost exactly
where she found it
                    in the yard in the dirt
                    in the grass in front of
the clump of fat-bud peonies.
She does not know the name, peony.

She does not know the name, stone.
She knows the stone by its gravity
its ironic taste its nameless
coloring

                And after seventy years
will visit, again, the ready way
the stone settled back into place,
unevenly, not as it had been,
not exactly   but satisfactorily,

to lodge untended in her memory
among other long-lived perennials.

THE FIRST, AT THE LAST

I

I walk home from the hospital useless
playing word-games in my head. Well,
I hadn't seen you in fifty-odd years.
You're the same. And, given
the sacred space of the dying,
you are different.

Your heart's a wreck.
"Sorry," the doctor said
in a modified paragraph.
You, old pilot, ceiling zero,
not smiling, muttered, "Grounded."

2

Word-games say: the groundlings
are the under
standers, keeping
their heads up
so they can see
feet first the actors
on the stage. They know
the Ghost must be
Will Shakespeare by his feet.
Their feet are tired
when Act V opens
at the level of their eyes.
They wait for it, silent,
throats swelled reactive

for utterance, understudying
the action of the Act
as scenes accumulate, words
gone once spoken but
not lost on groundlings
grounded & rooted
(since Act I asked its question)
by passions that build in them
to take in, to undertake
the final Act.

3

All he undertook
goes under, under
the undergrowth he rose from
fly-boy, lovely
in his day.
All his clothes
—spruce suit & tie—
are underclothes
against ungrounded grey.
All his studies understudy
an unstudied play.

> *Under the under*
> *of what I remember*
> *we are both twenty*
> *and except with each other*
> *underemployed.*

> *It is summer.*
> *Under our butter, bread,*
> *summer's hunger satisfied.*

RAIN ALL NIGHT, PARIS

On the road home the tide is rising.

Riding the road-tide is dangerous
but it's not safe to stand still.
Hang on the verge & you drown.

I'm going along for the ride.
I may see more riders further on.
Drowning must wait till I get there

and who knows who might be waiting
with a flashlight, a thermos,
even a raft or canoe.

Uncollected Poems, 1946–1971

A VISIT

Fine bitches all, and Molly Dance . . .

—DJUNA BARNES

Come for duty's sake (as girls do) we watch
The sly very old woman wile away from her pious
And stagger-blind friend, their daily split of gin.
She pours big drinks. We think of what
Has crumpled, folded, slumped her flesh in
And muddied her once tumbling blood that, young,
Sped her, threaded with brave power: a Tower,
Now Babel, then of ivory, of the Shulamite,
Collapsed to this keen dame moving among
Herself. She hums, she plays with used bright
Ghosts, makes real dolls, and drinking sings Come here
My child, and feel it, dear. A crooking finger
Shows how hot the oven is.

(Also she is alive with hate.
Also she is afraid of hell. Also, we wish
We might, illiberal, uncompassionate,
Run from her smell, her teeth in the dish.)

Even dying, her life riots in her. We stand stock still
Though aswarm with itches under her disreputable smiles.
We manage to mean well. We endure, and more.
We learn time's pleasure, catch our future and its cure.
We're dear blood daughters to this every hag, and near kin
To any after this of those our mirrors tell us foolishly envy us,
Presuming us, who are young, to be beautiful, kind, and sure.

(1946)

SENSIBILITY

"Cloth of true gold or Midas cloth chemically interchanged
Is beautiful but cold, does not drape well,
Cannot lend itself to every kind of color,
Has almost no, only a subtly ugly, smell.

Plant fibers take color like a good bride her man,
Taken and taken, giving and getting her fill
But like brides' solo mornings are fragrantly cool;
Drape with archaic stiffness, are best if held still.

(Silk was made to conform to the magical
Ambiance of worm to wings; its drape is vertical;
It's cool to touch, warm to wrap in; silk's special.)

Animals give us cloth incomparably whole, temperate,
Graceful, grateful in hand, keeping the weave and hue
We give it, better with use than when new."

The man who told me this grew
Anagogical nightmares dwarfed and askew
Under his pitiful iron bedstead, being mad;
But something of what he said was true.

(1947)

ST.-GERMAIN-DES-PRÉS:
Summer 1948

Crooked like all our ideas of ancient ascension
The abbey tower topples a little toward us in the haze,
Looking lightning-struck atop the quiet afternoon
Or perhaps visited by something toppling in other days.
Not now. Now grey, heavy, like a bank, the church
A house, is decorative and calm across the square,
Convenient for native weddings, funerals. From this cafe
It's handsome; it fits; smiling tourists recognize it there.

Now the ex-sergeant I've been drinking with has something
                                                    to say:
    ("Don't go in there, kid, I been, it's
    dangerous, no light what I call light but
    inside it's gold all over and the gold is going.
    I mean gold air goes blowing, there's an old
    sky blue altar up there too, don't let that gold
    air blow on you.")

                                                    (1948)

RITOURNELLE, FOR PARIS 1948

Down from the subtle grey Sorbonne and
Round the corner we come, to come
Into air moving, an altered air.
High, how bright, how the element of wings
Becomes something, swirls in
To some strong center near; it
Makes the peopled street stilly
Radiant: o here, see the magic
Magnet (it draws us): mimosa,
On sale in bunches from St.-Jean;
A sudden shudder of gold, a golden locus,
Branch-caught, a fog, all luminous,
Standing rush-bound in green tin cylinders
Before the sullen gay and selling
Paris face of the grey-cardiganed flower
Woman at the corner of Cluny.

With spring and the schools sleepless,
Alive and almost woman, I first now feel
Your intentions strike then dissipate
Marrying into my blood, sift drifting
Light-like everywhere.

The blown seen mimosa (we see it)
Blots up a shadow, all shadows, draws down
Light, is light's ripple, aura, echo,
Look, the little floral haze
Holds the whole tall air:

It blooms to illuminate
You in my bidden blood, you between
The Cluny garden and the flower
Woman, you in the human city, the human
City, you. And I take the banded branches
Brilliant from your hand.

(1949)

PRIVATE AND PROFANE

From loss of the old and lack of the new
From failure to make the right thing do
Save us, Lady Mary Wortley Montagu.
    From words not the word, from a feckless voice
    From poetic distress and from careless choice
    Exclude our intellects, James Joyce.
From genteel angels and apostles unappalled
From hollywood visions as virgins shawled
Guard our seeing, Grünewald.
    From calling kettle an existential pot,
    From bodying the ghost of whatever is not,
    John save us, o most subtle Scot.
From pace without cadence, from pleasures slip-shod
From eating the pease and rejecting the pod
Wolfgang keep us, lover of God.
    Couperin come with your duple measure
    Alter our minds against banal pleasure.
Dürer direct with strictness our vision;
Steady this flesh toward your made precision.
    Mistress of accurate minor pain,
    Lend wit for forbearance, prideless Jane.
From pretending to own what we secretly seek,
From (untimely, discourteous) the turned other cheek,
Protect our honor, Demetrius the Greek.
    From ignorance of structural line and bone
    From passion not pointed on truth alone
    Attract us, painters on Egyptian stone.
    From despair keep us, Aquin's dumb son;
    From despair keep us, Saint Welcome One;

From lack of despair keep us, Djuna and John Donne.
That zeal for free will get us in deep,
That the chance to choose be the one we keep
That free will steel self in us against self-defense
That free will repeal in us our last pretense
That free will heal us
    Jeanne d'Arc, Job, Johnnie Skelton,
    Jehan de Beauce, composer Johann,
    Dark John Milton, Charter Oak John
Strike deep, divide us from cheap-got doubt;
Leap, leap between us and the easy out;
Teach us to seize, to use, to sleep well, to let go;
Let our loves, freed in us, gaudy and graceful, grow.

(1950)

ANNIVERSARY

The big doll being broken and the sawdust fall
all scattered by my shoes, not crying
I sit in my dark to discover o failure annulled
opens out in my hands a purse of golden
salvaged sovereigns, from floors of seas culled.

The dancing doll split in an anguish and all
the cords of its elegant limbs unstrung; I
stumble whistling; the bones of my skull
marvelously start to sing, the whole shell
of myself invents without peril and contains a court aubade.

I hid the dovesmall doll but something found it. Frightened
I gave the fire what was left. Surrounding, it mulled
dulcet over the melting jeweled two blue eyes.
That night our hearth was desolate, but then its stones
sprung flowered and the soaring rafters arched.

Now all the house laughs, the sun shouts out clearly: dawn!
the sea owes us all its treasures; under the soft the riotous
explosion of our waking kiss or gift, a stone plucked or shorn
free of gravity falls upward for us, slow, and lies there, quietly.

(1951)

PLEASANT AVENUE

Is in Manhattan
As only those who live there know.

Even the paper-store man is
Italian, Gio. To him even
The *Daily News* delivery
Truckman is mannerly: he
Stops the truck, brings
The corded bundle of papers
Unripped in & sets it on
The maroon-grained plastic seat
Of the dim lunch counter's end stool.
Gio sells and smokes cigars.
I like to watch him unwrap one and
Light it, as if he were
Watching himself.
He sells us mothers malted milk by the
Big tin, cheap, good for li bambini, si.
Men of power gather in his store at night.
My life is so small I feel no fear of them.

The grocer down the block
And the grocer's glowing
Wife shaped like an earth-minder
Sell no potatoes, but stand beside a sea
Of kinds of greens; he lifts from beside
Parsley-tied bunches of uncrimped parsley
A head of escarole, thrusting its gold-to-pale

Center part up from among its shaggy green
To show me, Ecce, I behold.
Glad for his sake I approve. I buy.
His wife allows of me because my babies
Love the very smell of her, & do not whine;
So, nodding, smiling, nervous, he lets me choose
Pears one by one after I sniff at each bottom
Blossom-end to see if they're sweet yet. So far
I have not bruised any of his fruit; in his store
Insofar as I am correct, I am permissible.

East five blocks is the hard
Ware store, outside the invisible
Italian enclave. Here are
Ricani, the laughers; for them
I always wish to be darkly
Much prettier, and elegant.
A capella two men search dueting
For the cement nails I want; I read
Roach killer labels, ant killer
Labels, mouse and rat killer labels;
I glance at kinds of traps and wish
My city had room for more of the less
Desperately alive (despite us)
Withstanders-of-man. But next door
The bodega lady's parrot blazes
Green and thrives!

Brakes on Lexington screech as the
Bodega lady scolds the knife-eyed gang-
Boys and they shuffle; she dares
Send them home to their mothers, sí
Sí sí sí sí sí sí, and they go,
Laughing. I'm not afraid of them either.
I have nothing to fear from them

Being I guess afraid only of the loss of love
And of hurting children. And so here
I have nothing to fear.

(1952)

"VILLE INDIGÈNE":
Afrique du Nord

Amazed in a garden shut high
In a cliff-caught city beautifully
Clear above the ocean and the sea,
High with a private love
You and I
Watch the processional one young Arab
Waiter come on attentive feet,
His apparent focus of balance our
Pleasure at his copper tray and tea.
Tea is at last not English but
Oriental, hot-mint, hot-sweet,
Indigenous to this graceful, mosaic-
Divided oblong of garden
Built to shelter princes at their
Ceremonies, built to shunt aside
The burnt-out streaming desert wind.
The royal garden's public now, though
Empty today of tourists save for our dazzled in-
Ranging love, high over the great waters,
Close within color-crowded walls,
Directly under the moving sky.

If we are visitors yes it is beautiful.
Madame est américaine? Madame est
Américaine. We all three smile. His formal
Waiter's garment is a blur of white
Against the semi-distant blurs
Of the big-clustered orange blue or
Violet blossoming vines. His robes

Are subtle. They move as softly as
The subtle walled-off wind stirs.
What inhabits him, however, is very still.

Against a blaze-blue sky blaze-white
Ungainly storks flash gloriously.
We're so high they seem to stoop to drop
Below us as they slide
In a majesty of omen-holding wing-spread
Into flight from rooftops level with our eyes.
When perched, they stand, contre-jour
Angled against all the sky, cut
Out, in an evidence of light. It is
Beautiful. Sight, seeing this, is satisfied.
The rampant streets criss-cross, man-wide,
Up to here, violet-shadowed, beautiful.
With wild voices in prayer-shrill
Shadows beggars beautifully sing.
(It is God's act in you that they beseech.)
Flat white facades, mosaic-set, inscript,
Diminish, play back, enhance the sun
Into a beautiful distraction of tipped
Uninhabitable inhabited planes. Here each one
Is one; and is so most beautifully.

Even the root-of-violet black
Stinking ribbon of sewer guttering down the
Stone street sides is beautiful. Women
Columnar in white djellabas
Are each beautiful; at work, old, burdened;
Pregnant, at work, giggling together;
Little girls, quick at their work. Emancipated
Young women, buttoncd into groundlength grey
Gowns by two hundred and twenty grey buttons,
Go gloved, masked, and slippered in sun red or

Cyclamen, fierce blue or green, with a chic
I must envy and a ribbonsupple movement
So beyond my angularity that envy flees.
A splendid people, beautifully moving in their
Beautiful city, courteous to quiet visitors.

If we are not visitors but persons here;
If these sewers are my sewers, these sere
Exhausted men my men, these loneliest
Bearers of burdens my suffering women;
Their fairy-tale handful of lentils and old dates
My daily food; their ignorance mine
(As these are all mine and these strangers
All my blooded close relations though
Understanding's denied us and communication's
Impossible no matter what the tongue)
If I am these beggars and I am,
It is not less beautiful but my
Eyes are blistered by it
So that they cannot (love, keep
Me constant, us alive) (my peace is
I swear whatever where
You and I kissing stand
My head between your heavy hands
But we are now somewhere neither
Of us understands) cannot see. My eyes
That in this city cannot claim to see
Are beggar's eyes infected by this
Anguish, by these my
Deaths and marriages that I know
Are not ever to be
Known nor even
Wept by me.

(1953)

SAM REFUTED, RESPECTFULLY

Experience can't teach
What some are born knowing:
How comely it is to be,
Dreamily, what you're
Likely taken for—

But pray it teaches you
Never to keep score.

Few of us ever do
Get used to
Using as we're being
Used by (I don't)
Or used to seeing
That, apple or knuckle,
My is not I—
And only a saint won't
Now and then ignore why
Yours is not you.

Sam Johnson kicked
The stone of a stone,
Scraped his shoe
And his ankle bone,
And did not care
For he alone then
Had proved anew
Fair and square
That he alone to

Him alone was
Usable, true,
And there.

(1954)

TAKE ANY CARD

Take any card; if we agree
in the beginning that Elohim
can mean chosen then we may be
tranquil partners, unopposed,
uncommitted, gaming
as we join to regard
our cards how they cluster
like Eve's beasts come to naming
patient and innocent
urgently being themselves.

It is your turn. Take a card,
one at a time, one of mine,
      or any one,

and the Sun
explodes all over again
something crystalline happens
grows crowded with colors
goes blue-green and green;
somewhere too remote,
something too small to be seen
too lost and common in the deep
for the first time stops drifting
stands against the current
and moves of its own accord.

For these cards are words and unlock
possible tricks into becoming new

species of victories. We can afford
to allow words meaning, as a double gamble
because from the center of the circle
the whole pack is visible
and whatever card you take
may well be a chosen one.

(1955)

UNDER A ROUTINE PROCEDURE

Intelligent and kind often, hands, I can't count them,
About and upon me, now soar worse than dreams of scissors,
So many gifted hands gone huge with threat, the stars
Above the blood-haze making a warning pattern
In the divisive signals of an alien script, in a tongue
Dead as the downstreet tree whose roots, believe me,
Thrust and crawl deep. I too am obedient.
You are not admitted here yet.

    I say I fear I mean I love as I was
    Taught to fear and love and taught myself
    To exchange them both for you.

Relieved, you go. My thought seeks not that for comfort
But what once pleasured me; I remember such things well.
The harelipped anaesthetist leans dear and safe
Saying Hush, and Soon now. Someone else said Rest now.
Flashing. Arched above me. Bitter honey, insulted body.
You too? How much, which, of what some she did, do you
Do again at my quick yes? I'll never know. Revenge
Is in the vice versa, lover; laugh. I go under laughing.

At dawn knives and bottles are back on steel shelves.
I am back in the dim ward. I see the river. City boats scud.
We are simpler, Confucius, left to our urban selves,
Than the rain-forest people. Our temple
Has an altarstone and our altarstone sweats blood.

(1956)

ELEGY FOR ELIZABETH BLEECKER AVERELL

Abrupt as that blessing gesture you always made
when we met or went our ways, you've bravely fled
lonely as ever, and no more than usual afraid,
beyond us, Elizabeth, abruptly dead.

Outside, birdsharp songs sprinkle the seagreen grass;
small-leaved trees sparkle with birds in June light in sea air.
You're not kneeling here. This is your Requiem Mass.
We kneel; you triumph; your absence strains our sight.
Even later your sons, even grown, won't know how fair
how tall as bridal, vivid, their young young mother was.

Your hard grace, your handsome, hurt-taught
body that made much of much delight,
your flashing sun-bound head,
with you are dead.

In life you were merciful, loved
all degrees of subtle enemies, I
among them who sure I loved you did
not cherish you, and so now cry.
Elizabeth who living was courteous, was merry day by day,
glorious friend, befriend me beyond death;
show us who do not love or know love enough or go love's way
your now love without limit, please, Elizabeth

(1957)

GIGUE FOR CHRISTMAS EVE

"O woman, go gently; the beast is too old
To get up a trot when his belly is cold
—Poor creature; your own, if the truth must be told
Is as tight as a drum and how long can it hold?"

"I forgot him, good Joseph; forgive me, now do.
Go easy, poor donkey; I forgot about you
With my thinking we'd soon get some village in view.
Do you take your own time, now, the night is still new."

"Man dear are you mad?" the beast whispered aside.
"Far worse heels than hers have belabored my side!
Why, the woman you mention is God's own good bride
And I'm honored to have her along for the ride."

"Don't I know it," said Joseph. "But don't let her hear.
I say, 'Pity the donkey,' to capture her ear.
For herself she won't spare, and it's that that I fear
With the jog in this road that might bring her down here."

"O good Joseph! No wonder God made you her man!
Your respect for her nature's a pleasure to scan.
Now if God speed me easy, I'll run the whole span
And get you to Bedlam, according to plan!"

Well, the donkey's brave words woke twelve angels at least;
Four and twenty wings feathered the speed of the beast,
Till in Bedlam his burden was gently released
Just in time for the star that roared out of the east.

(1958)

TO FORBID GRIEF

Let her be. She ran a long way,
the hunting pack at her heels.
She ran from dawn to past noonday
before the pack at her heels.

The hunters never came near her
even at the last.
The end of desire dared her
and she did not let it past.

From dark to deep brightness gone,
from racing to rest,
we may not idly mourn
her whose brightness blessed.

Let her quit body be
whose light runs free.

(1959)

BECAUSE WE CERTAINLY HAVE
NOTHING BETTER TO DO

Applaud the man of extremest scholarship
inspecting the mysteries of his fellow
subway passengers, whose habitual love lifts
his eyes from his book to take in the loud trip

Make a feast for the
tireless walker, the girl who paints
difficult pictures, who wanders so
strictly, responsibly looking and as
canny as the surest of the saints

Praise the anguished world that also holds
the ironic survivor the gentle
retired from business man
among his geraniums and neighbors,
an example of carefulness, gladness,
with his wife, both self-effacing,
in the supermarket, the polling-place.

Let us less wise than these
praise our power to
value their victories.

(1960)

SURVIVAL

Watching you strike worldly poses flirting
Excited with someone's arch French wife
While I converse about roses (Shakespeare,
Sappho, Eliot, Bowen, Yeats; they are in
Theophrastus; our gardens have aphids
Climbers and chromatic fugues) surrounded
By cups, coffee, cakes, the sleeping
Children's wooden toys, I seven months
Pregnant for the seventh time
Disappear

(1961)

SPRINGING

In a skiff on a sunrisen lake we are watchers.

Swimming aimlessly is luxury, just as walking
loudly up a shallow stream is.

As we lean over the deep well, we whisper.

Friends at hearths are drawn to the one warm air;
strangers meet on beaches drawn to the one wet sea.

What wd it be to be water, one body of water
(what water is is another mystery). (We are
water divided.) It wd be a self without walls,
with surface tension, specific gravity, a local
exchange between bedrock and cloud of falling and rising,
rising to fall, falling to rise.

(1962)

DIALOGUE OF NEMO AND PERSONNE

"Are you still nice to sleep with?
Do you snore?"

    "I'm so precise to leap with, that
    I'm twice as nice to peak with, and
    if I snored my every snort would make you, lady,
    like me more."

"But can I count on you to wake me
up on time?"

    "I've listened for your laughing in my
    history of gardens. I can help you
    list the whispers of the paths where dreaming takes you.
    You have only to agree and,
    I guarantee,
    yes, I'll wake you up on time."

"I'm visible here but I must be
anonymous along my periphery.
My garden shuts out noone, it does no harm.
But where I laugh, or whisper, you may not take stock.
I praise but do not need you. I've set the alarm.
I trust my own clock."

"Though not proud you are not kind.
Though I'll keep us in my mind, Marie,
it may well be better for me
that you go free.
If you call that free."

(1963)

EXPLICATION DE TEXTE

Before spring began,
On a day ice melted early
The explorers' Samoyedes ran
Barking their laughing bark
Wild with February pleasure,

And came back yipping, nunciates:

They had found
What we all look for, treasure,

As if new-killed, a mastodon,
On a tilt of tundra
At the glacier's lip.

To it they had bayed their men proudly
Over the hard wet ground to show
The food mountain, the beast
Flash-frozen by surprise
A million melting springs ago;
Caught while cropping grass,
Its flesh still fresh,
Its great organs preserved perfectly.
With it were found
A fringe of benefits, dangling
From the Playland man-tall jaws:
Grasses now extinct and still golden
Buds and flowers of uncrushed
Marsh marigold,
Eons old.

Knowledge of these facts
Came to me painlessly
Via a *Reader's Digest* I read
Waiting on a wooden chair to see
The good J. Spivak, M.D.;
I think they mean:
That mammoths ate marigolds.
That dogs are clever.
That cold is a mystery.

I think they mean that despite
Odds and ills which defy even a keen
Diagnostician, despite
How readers digest how
Reader's Digest writers write
Up Life's Adventurous Perhaps,

Despite the lazy bowels, gin breath,
Wronged things, sick souls,
Murder, life at its worst,

Life came first, not death.
Despite you death
Life comes first

(1964)

THE CROW DRESSED IN PEACOCK FEATHERS
(Le Geai Paré des Plumes du Paon)

A peacock cast its feathers. A passing crow saw,
    And stuck them in among his own;
He swore their cock-eyed glory was home-grown,
    And walked out grand from crup to caw.
Real peacocks looked twice, and shrieking at his deceit
    Pecked, plucked, beaked until in defeat
He sought his own. The crows, shocked by his wild, wrecked
                  state,

Thought him a foreigner and forced him to retreat.
    Some peacock crows circulate
On two feet, decked out in cast-offs of others' brains;
They are known as plagiarists by these ill-got gains.
    Enough said. I do not design
To cause these people any further harm or pain.
    Theirs is no business of mine.

Translated from the French of Jean de La Fontaine,
Fables, Book IV, 9.

(1965)

A TALE TOLD BY ATHENEUS
(VENUS CALLIPYGUS)
(Conte Tirée D'Athenée [Venus Callipyge])

Two sisters of ancient Greece both laid claim
To the finest, fairest rear of their time.
Which tail forged ahead? Which bottom's true fame
Topped? Which back was in front, which terce most prime?
A judge chose the elder girl's back matter;
Her finish was more fine and far matter.
She got the prize, and his heart; soon they wed.
"But the younger's sitter's not a smatter
Less meet; I'll marry her," his brother said.
It went so well, their joys were so perfected,
That after them a temple was erected
In honor of Venus Callipygus.
No other church— though I don't know its rite—
Could so, from head to epididymis,
Move me with deep devotion to its site.

Translated from the French of Jean de La Fontaine,
Contes, Part I, 6.

(1966)

SYMPOSIUM HOLIDAY

Out of the sky I fell onto a little island
Ireland; without the Yes of the dame up from Gib,
and only nod's knowledge of Dedalus,

with a family name from Blake's day and
a bookish hope for heroines (bookish)
I dropped in on Dublin to my embarrassment.

Such treasure, such honor, such gold, so many
sea-sprung bright-spoken women & men! A woman
feels like a fooled harpy in the wrong pub, though.

Among those who permit themselves mutual courtesy
I came unready as a booted crusader crude on
the carpets of the silken King of Jerusalem;

they praised my step. With kind mockery they fed me
as if I were included. For desirable as well as
kniving speech is current among them, word-drunk or sober.

No Roman Law, no Industrial Devolution: God save us,
Joyce was right! the Phoenix lives—here!
I fear lèse-majesté. Someone, please tell the Irish

and make it stick, that their inability to imitate
their beauty need not humble them into pride,
nor their skill as vivisectionists.

(1967)

LAST RESORT

Admit me to the circle of light.
Out here the jackals snuffle
Where, I thought, lions ranged before.

I hear you coming. You unlock the door.
You do admit me, though last time
I left fast, left you baffled.

We make love and other excuses.
The air's rank. There's sand on the floor.
Between the walls a nestful of squirrels
Scuffles, mewing.

Jackals have their uses.

(1968)

"LUXURIA," DREAMBOAT

A small ship, but I can't board her—
where she sails the water's always cold,
choppy, its currents unpredictably
treacherous.

If I owned her, I might. But I can't afford her;
her price jumps ten percent each time she's sold
& she wasn't cheap when she belonged to me or you
or what wrecked both of us.

(1969)

HALF FULL

outside in
grief rage grey pain
bright pain
this is it the
worst cold spring
lost tired with too much to do
no time to fix the garden
no money
no friend
a pain in the gut
no good love
this is it the
bleak hurting year
I guess a lot of years
got me in to.

at noon of the long day
flat out taking time to catch my breath
under the butterfly drift
of apple petals I see the many
spears and heads of perennials
coming up! strong green
well I even see
lots of buds on that delicate
difficult old gorgeously
fireflowered
peony tree

(1970)

OUT OF THE NORTH: TWO VIEWS

I

"Though I come
In this eagle's disguise
     dolent, dolent, soaring indolently,
     equating the weight of my body with
     the width of my wings so as to ease
     in a wide side-slipping spiral down
     toward the edge of the ring of trees,
though I address you
with eagle calls and cries

I am a giant really and you therefore
should love me since although you
claim you are a falcon, believe me,
you are a giant, too."

2

"What I might well say
    will go unsaid
    though it whistle away
    inside my head.
Though you are eagle to my falcon eyes
And think us sons of morning in disguise

though neither nest nor monster made us

and although I know what you forget,
that we are a god's get; more, the space who begot us
never forgot us and never betrayed us,

I a falcon feel only the umbrel flow
of warm air mounting through this cooler hour,
streaming steadily up from the hollow of trees,
pressing under the wings of my venturesome body,
upholding your body and its imperial power.

What else I have to add
no one will hear from me.
What creature would not be glad
to scorn disguises, to see
with falcon sight your eagle urgency,
and to be what he seems to be?"

(1971)

From *True Minds*, 1956

TAKE MY DISPROPORTIONATE DESIRE

Enough of expressionist flowers lions and wheat,
Let us consider our separate needs
Here in this beautiful city of delicate surfaces
That a touch makes bleed.

Bring me that truth love-ridden whose black blaze makes
A comfort in the ice-bitten ghettos of cities, that wise
Love whose intemperate told truth thrusts into the aching
Arms of old men old women's lonely bodies with a cry.

All lovers, even lucky, need such intransigence as stays
Wrecked harborers who together cough, drink, spit
Gay blood into the gutter. I need that passion, miracle,
Incautious faith. To only you I offer it.

"QU'AI-JE À FAIRE EN PARADIS?"

Alexander did not in god's costume recall more
Disquietly Macedonian apples and tame snakes than I,
Fantastically shod with peace and cloaked with love,
Evoke old names for bitterness and hear harsh ghosts cry.

The Persians mocked, though they knelt, his leopard and
golden
Skirts and slotted crown that claimed the holy stood
After voyages among their halls. What kneelers laugh
To see me upright here, having cast off sword and hood?

MATINS & LAUDS

Excited as a sophisticated boy at his first
Passion of intellect, aware and fully free
Having lost title to full liberty; struck
Aware, for once, as I would always be;

It day and I still shaken, still sure, see
It is not ring-magic nor the faithing leap of sex
That makes me your woman; marks our free
And separate wills with one intent; sets
My each earlier option at dazzling apex
And at naught; cancels, paid, all debts.
Restless, incautious, I want to talk violence,
Speak wild poems, hush, be still, pray grace
Taken forever; and after, lie long in the dense
Dark of your embrace, asleep between earth and space.

POSSESSION

You are right. In dreams I might well dance before the Ark.
Coming out of ether I might cry on reed and rood of
                                        sacredness.
Yet you should not for that reason suspect altars between us
Nor scent a fear of incense in the cruciform caress.
Marriage is blessed but does not bless.

I warned you before this smoked ground struck your knees,
Saying Be holy, see where the whipped top spins;
Saying This world is that world's mimesis, bloodless
But sensual and we do not even contain our sins.
I said, Betray it and the bedraggled cockerel wins.

Listen. Do you hear? Now he crows.
Now we are going where God knows.

Come to term the started child shocks
Peace upon me; I am great with peace;
Pain teaches primal cause; my bones unlock
To learn my final end. The formal increase
Of passionate patience breaks into a storm of heat
Where calling on you love my heart's hopes rise
With violence to seize as prayer this sweet
Submitting act. I pray. Loud with surprise
Thrown sprung back wide the blithe body lies
Exultant and wise. The born child cries.

COMMUNION OF SAINTS:
The Poor Bastard Under the Bridge

The arrows of the narrow moon flock down direct
Into that looking heart by Seine walls unprotected.
Moonward the eyes of that hurt head still will
Stare and scarcely see the moonlight spill
Because black Notre-Dame between her towers
Strikes home to him the third of this day's hours
And he, now man, heaped cold afaint
Below the Pont Marie will, with a shout,
Enlist among the triumphant when Poor Saint
Julien's bells will clock out
Four.
      In his rags, unchapleted, almost astray
Among the dead packed all immaculate away
Under the city, he awaits his sentry
The four o'clock moon to warrant for his entry
                       o and pure
The pure in children's ranks by bells immured
In gowns of light will singing telling rise
Unfold their arms impelled without surprise
Will lift up flowered laurel, will walk out
Among their golden singing like a victor's shout
To their triumphant heaven's golden ringing brim
And welcome welcome welcome him.

" 'WHAT ARE YOU DOING HERE, STEPHEN?' "

Joyce, *Ulysses*

Lean walkers on light feet connive
At splendor, fail, get by another chance
Truth's best children, though bastard, born alive,
Born rehearsing the modes of need, the sleeping dance.
Before the pivotal altar, between bright horn and holy horn,
Step the cherished, cheating innocents, sweetly stepping,
                                          capricorn.
They improvise to flute them, who have gone too far:
The instructed musicians, responsible, are their servants
                                          secular.

Moving always, and wary, making an arc
Across straight streets, shy at shadow or post,
Half-halting, half-smiling, breathless, they hark.
These kneeling think ellipses, square the circled host,
Rise heavy and gaudy with wine, a new pain held in the head;
They go out graceful and laborless, greeding, easy, capriped.

They feed them, pouring, whose own thirst shuts their throats:
Impatient waiters, forfeit in their many-colored paid-for coats.

ROCKEFELLER THE CENTER

Roland is dead and the ivory broken
Marie has forgotten the limb-striking end of joy.

    Pigeons patter, whirr, at the copy cathedral; a Prometheus
    Aeschylus did not intend submits to sparrows,
                          less than ever free;
    At his manufactured feet the delicate ice-skaters swirl.

    A paralleled curve incised among angles, the splendid
                                      loose
    Avenue ripples with peopled cars, and the figuring girl
    Looks at the sky beyond the sidewalk's ginkgo tree.

Though the sea-coves echo with innumerable
Voices no man suspects the vanished Neirids.

Artemis at midnight is
No longer solicited.

From *Admit Impediment*, 1981

FOR A DIVORCE

I

Death is the price of life.
Lives change places.
            Asked why
we ever married, I smile
and mention the arbitrary fierce
glance of the working artist
that blazed sometimes in your face

but can't picture it;

I do recall (1) shoes you left
in my closet, echoing worn-out
Gauguin; (2) how once under down
drugs I roared at you Liar! oh liar!
exulting in not lying
                ((as if
I'd made a telltale drawing . . .)

2

How dear how undark appear the simple
apparently simple wishes of the untried will;
how dark it is here and how
suddenly too still.

3

Glad I need not chance again
against your prone packed weight
my uncertain stance,
I giddy with relief
relax into mobility.

The state we made of love,
that you fled out of
empty-handed,
I have enlarged
into a new mainland geography
where I move as if unburdened where
my burdens bear me.
You said once I had
taught you human speech.
I am glad
I never taught you to dance.

4

Or, perhaps I drove you to flight.
Perhaps (freckled) islanded
I (skinny) was Circe;
Aiaia sounds familiar and
even on my crystal sands even
under my fragrant trees you
were a pig

a pig, and I a Circe stupefied who
could not tell the master from the man,
tusk-torn because too slow to know
I had in choosing you

dismissed Odysseus
and the luck of Odysseus and
his mind immune to magic

for a prentice hand the sea could tame,
a poor sailor, lotus changeling, destined
never to come home.

. . . or so let me flatter myself,
fabulously.

5

But if the fable go that way, it goes on,
to say that in myths gross beasts must
wound; it is their work; by this work
mere moon-starred magicians may turn in
to useful plainer day's-eye citizens
          and so, that blind
          boar whose tusks wound
          becomes a cruel kind
of guide or christ, an unwilling
saviour, greedy to the hurt that,
necessary, healed to a shiny scar,
serves to teach
identify or save.
And should this be the case
I wish I could say I'd rendered you such grace.

6

          (. . . a drawing telltale
& pure as one of yours when you drew edged

objects—a bird, a wheel—in the shift
of the light they turn in; as you drew
the soft unpierced air that bore
sounds of wings and waters at Banyuls
where we sunstruck went up under the arch
where we came upon fountains))
                    and now
exactly I do
darkly I do
          recall the you of then when
every time you touched me it was true.

7

Deaths except for amoeba articulate
life into lives, separate, unnamed, new.
Not all sworn faith dies. Ours did.
(1) I am now what I now do.
(2) Then in me
that stunning lover
                    was you.

BASIC SKILLS

Crazy chopped shrieks of school
people penned in the scarred
yard stop at the metal
whistle blown hard.

Exposed among monitors, at
angles marked in the cement,
the children shrink. Teaching
screaming & cringing, the raw
teacher screams above
a selected 8-year-old boy.

What's outside the shiny
web fence is invisible,
unofficial, its random strengths
—natural hugs, curious energy,
all that only age of gold—
for these lead-alchemic hours gone
into the jailsteel boundary
taken in & glinting
like tears behind eyes he shuts, as
the head of the boy goes down.

RESIDUAL PARALYSIS

FOR JUNE JORDAN

I'm an unable woman who loves to dance
but my polio leg won't go, or will
a while, until yanked by muscle cramps
that grip the ankle so it gives way
& locks twisted, perpendicular. And then
of course the damned thing's sprained, fat, blue, & wrong.

When I hear music I think nothing's wrong
that I can't manage, and I start to dance,
inside at first, smiling for the beat; then
the sound strides up my back & claims it will,
if I let it, float me safe all the way
on the long waves of high style nothing cramps.

So I'm a chump, surprised, betrayed by cramps,
ashamed to admit I have something wrong
until it's too late & rhythm drains away.
Let drop, I fall untuned outside the dance
insulted in the body of the will
to hold control, that cooled my fever then.

That I was sick, I kept half secret then.
Years of vanity, vain practice, vain cramps
got me walking even downstairs at will.
I valued that, my false claim, "Nothing's wrong!
(I can't press down a clutch and I can't dance
but) I'm not lame (not very, anyway)."

Lies have small voice when dancing has its way;
old true tales sweeten into the now of then
which is the breathing beat of every dance;
the wrecks & twists of history uncramp
into trust that present kindness can't go wrong
among warm partners of a common will.

I try. If I can stop lying, I will.
I'll claim my cramps & limit them that way,
trust and forget my history, right & wrong,
while others dance. I might, less vain than then,
forgive dead muscles and relax their cramps.
I can love dancing from outside the dance.

When trust uncramps the ordinary will
to laugh its way past accidental wrong,
those outside then step inside the dance.

ABOUT MY BIRTHDAY

I'd like to assume
from my April birthday,
I quickened the womb
on the 4th of July.

If you suffered as I
a sternly fought tendency
to endless dependency
you'd know why.

BILINGUAL

Languages before they are words
or systems are persons speaking
and persons spoken to. The bilingual
cannot, for example, convey in English,
"Au placard, la lavande
fait bien blanchir les linges";
there's no American woman to whom
it could be said.

The pain of having two languages comes from a
straining between them in the mind,
from a need to keep them separate and
a desire, forbidden, dangerous,
to marry them: like twins who
safely unentwined by each other's presence
stress their differences
and who when absent cannot but represent
longing for union of the purest kind.

The two tongues must be untrue to each other.
Their speaker always has one mute mouth kept pressed
closed against the barrier and already possessed
of other words to word each word better,
that the speaking one is deaf to.

Dreams give relief but no rest.
Both babble there, each other's audience,
making love eloquent at last, coupling
with the rich attention grand passion

gives in slowness to the body of the lover;
there the American answers, with pleasure,
"I love the smell of lavender."

AMONG WOMEN

What women wander?
Not many. All. A few.
Most would, now & then,
& no wonder.
Some, and I'm one,
Wander sitting still.
My small grandmother
Bought from every peddler
Less for the ribbons and lace
Than for their scent
Of sleep where you will,
Walk out when you want, choose
Your bread and your company.

She warned me, "Have nothing to lose."

She looked fragile but had
High blood, runner's ankles,
Could endure, endure.
She loved her rooted garden, her
Grand children, her once
Wild once young man.
Women wander
As best they can.

FROM THE FOUNTAIN AT VAUCLUSE

I

This light is water. In emerald ascent
Pooled at the cliff it has chiseled, it has brought
To light its clear, unsounded affluent.
To its star-planet I am astronaut
Come home. Crowds come with me, intent
On holiday at the Fountain of Vaucluse.
Its vulnerable air brings us up short.

A girl dips her foot in, holding her shoes.
A boy throws stones so splashes distort
The pool; most males do, as if they confuse
Marking with marring; as if, innocent,
Inept at awe, they smash what they can't use
Or ignore, here where joy's intelligent
In the still light bodied by greening blues.

2

My heart steadies here, sensing something taught:
I take this pool holding opening as
The font and vulva of the planet, brought
From depth to light by the soft force it has
And from view to vision by the path it wrought,
Unknown, central, central, earth-old, blue, blue.
They nod to see it, women on the grass:
Some cross the crown of sun-lit stone it wells up through
To watch how limpidly it lets light pass
Transparent to itself. Girls stare who,

Women-trained not to catch but to be caught,
Are not able to shout, throw, sprawl askew.
Here, their malfunction works in them like thought
Transcending the loss of all they do not do.

3

Or so it seems, as girls without parade
Bend to the shoreline, cup their hands, and drink.
Two old women hand themselves down and wade.
Some girls with brothers throw stones; most shrink
As the waters break. They may be afraid
Of breaking anything: *and that is right*
Though praise for it negates what are, we think,
The claims of power. As woman, I take fright
At power in brute strength (here at the blue brink
Of star-borne paradise) which breeds the fight
I shirk but know my people can't evade
While the good, self-bound in either covert spite
Or child-like impotence, watch their good fade.
Landscape be my lens. Rectify my sight.

4

Cockerel, brash, these July boys & men
Cannot love what they have never seen
Or see what pecking greed keeps hid from them,
Trained not to listen for what their lives mean
But to beat. By that blinding stratagem
All lose. Women and men confuse success
With loud failure to work and work serene.
Boys we raise to thrive under cockpit stress,
Faced here with peaceful force, must intervene.

A child trammeled in heeled shoes and ironed dress
Smiles for the blue pool, climbs close to it; then
Her hand if timid touches its face. Yes
I hate her heels and pleats. But praise is sudden
In me for her easy move of tenderness.

5

Another male; three stones; but though I wince
I see what their opposite costs my sons.
They pay high for their gentle difference
From the mindless strength of competition;
Yet even now I am not convinced
That I was wrong (now that they rightly see
Weakness as tyranny, and have begun
To search themselves for true strength, desperately)
To hate unimagining ambition
Which says, "I'll be more," not, "Here's what I'll be."
A worse mistake I have regretted since:
My daughter was not taught priority
For her own work.
       Could I wash out those prints,
How, how could I now teach them differently?

6

Some women can see only males, and some
See only themselves, as if they too were male.
Both own the bitter equilibrium,
The base, hurt power of slaves. They are the frail
Employers of pity; they are dumb,
Cute, weak at will.
       My daughter did not learn

Those tricks. She neither flirts nor wails.
Generous & gentle, can she stand firm
Having found her own ground, or will she fail
(I've failed) to use her time and too late turn
To lay her claim? Can her young wisdom
Keep loving-kindness and yet rise to spurn
Unsuitable self-sacrifice?
       Now come
Two sisters to the pool where water burns.

7

The air above the sun-flamed pool is air
Changing into freshness. The two girls face
The subtle water. One sighs. Both stare
As if the split of mind from will were effaced
At last, by the freshening. They, laughing there,
Are the generation of the world. I see
Women may model a fresh human grace
That is not weak but deep for those set free
Of win & lose, and—present like this place—
Come from depth to breadth by pressing steadily.

A tall old woman whispers, *de bon aire,*
"Paradisa esta si." Is? Was? Not to me?
I'm confused. Her words startle everywhere.
Daughter, your paradisa is not; may be.

GHOST WRITER

Irene on my tiny list of answers to despair
I star your name

But now I come to complain.
Lately, you only ghostwrite.
Able, serviceable, conscript
Papers on liverfluke or cattlebone,
Speeches on green research phrased
For a larynx not your own,
Replace in your portfolio the work
I think you were born to,
The personal words.
You have stopped writing those shapes
That leave calm people
            dizzy with listening to
            your truthful speakers
            say their human tunes.

Sensual, intellectual, acute to differentiate:
Sweet realist, you have always ghostwritten
What you can of what you cannot tolerate.
Strange to what sounds stupid
            you light-wristed
Transmute as you catch them
Our banal verbal moves into
        dazzles of juggled idea;
I am a bore but you are not bored; you
Fox me into surprises, for

You ghostwrite your friends too:
As you imagine how we act toward who we are
You better us;
You hear us
         and, entirely pleasant
         in earrings and a silk disguise,
         you glance at the glass you hold,
         you think, fast, speak,
             smile,
         swallow your drink,
And we see what you see we mean.
Then for the pleasures you give us
    you thank us
So discreetly we accept your thanks.

Grace, as it dilates, effaces.
Is this how you become yourself?

You do become yourself.
Even your shy ankles are articulate of it;
Your hair no matter who cuts it is
Crisp as tulips and suits you; your
Voice, when you speak in it, is
Unmistakable, a rationale for words.
        I catch
As it vanishes that chaste voice,
Behind the words, in years of pageants
You wrote for the children for holidays
—lost once played: daylilies, champagne, ephemera:
    Bastille Day birthday high jinks,
    a mime for a dancing giant,
    Noah's arksong, solstice jokes,
    now lost,
Matches written to be lit and lost—

You interrupt in your delicate French,
Its irony delicate, "Je regrette . . ."

Yes I regret your lost writing, the woodland
Dry its streams re-directed, the stories
Left random, left unsaved,
Your sightseeing left unrecorded, lost,
Your language lent.
Yes yet
      no, I take back my complaint.

      I praise your Maygames
      your short always festivals
      their blaze-and-black fireworks,
      the confident gesture of them
      their formidable innocence.
The genius you modulate into helpful use thrives
      despite you,
      as the haunt of your lost lines
      improves your children into celebrants,
        your friends into imagined action,
        me into asking
If perhaps a woman
So rich is so free
She can
Sun-brilliant, sun-unseen,
Afford to keep
Herself like a secret, Irene,
And the secret, meekness
      unspeakable
      sanctity

THE DIFFÉRANCE: CHATOU-CROISSY

It was hard, but she was doing it,
Raising him well, the boy
Fathered on her by her mother's lover—
Buying his shoes in brand-name stores
Where fitting took time, keeping his teeth good.
Her skills were domestic, the knife
In her small hands all edge as it flashed
Rabbit flesh, parsley, leeks,
Into sizes she wanted.
When she could, she married a steady boy
Who'd never thought to get so fine a woman,
Who got on with her son,
Who even loved the boy though ashamed of him.

"Yes," she said, "he's of course the boss.
Whatever he says to do
I do, he loves to see me do it,
I never say a word. But now you're married,
I can tell you. Listen, let him be the boss,
Call him boss, all day,
Even in bed, do it his way,
Why not, *ça ne coute rien,* and
He's got to sleep sometime:
That's your chance. Every night I wait till he snores,
Then I just lean my elbow into him until
He has to turn, a minute later I just lean
Again, he turns, you see? It's not for nothing
He's got pits of shadows all around his eyes,

The punk. You'll see, you can call him boss,
Boss all day, he'll eat it up,
Late at night, he never knows, you laugh."

LIVE MODEL

Who wouldn't rather paint than pose—
Modeling, you're an itch the artist
Doesn't want to scratch, at least
Not directly, and not yet.
You think, "At last, a man who knows
How bodies are metaphors!" (You're wrong.)

First time I posed for him he made
A gilded throne to sit me on
Crowned open-armed in a blue halfgown.
I sat his way, which was not one of mine
But stiff & breakable as glass,
Palestill, as if
With a rosetree up my spine.
We had to be speechless too,
Gut tight in a sacring thermal
Hush of love & art;
Even songs & poems
Were too mundane for me to quote
To ease our grand feelings
So I sat mute, as if
With a rosetree down my throat.

Now I breathe deep, I sit slack,
I've thrown the glass out, spit,
Evacuated bushels of roses.
I've got my old quick walk
& my big dirty voice back.

Why do I still sometimes sit
On what is unmistakably like a throne?
Why not. Bodies are metaphors
And this one's my own.

HALF-LIFE:
Copies to All Concerned

Gentlemen: how are you? Here things go well.
I write you after these many years to ask
If you have any news of all I lost
That I'd forwarded to you, insured, I'd thought,
First Class, on urgent demand, with a good
Guarantee (though that would be expired now).

What I miss is not you (as you do, now?)
But the girl I gave you. Did she do well,
That stern young person planning to be good,
Sure of her dress, her footing, her right to ask?
Lovers have half-life in each other's thought
Long after; is the mark she made quite lost?

Have you traces of her? That she got lost
I'd never guessed; but from what I hear now,
You never quite received her, though we thought
She knew more than the directions well
And would get by, skilled in what not to ask.
Were her efforts at lipstick any good?

Did she learn to tell bad eagerness from good?
If you do remember her, then she's not lost;
I've forgotten her so long, I must ask
(I didn't love her then as I might now)
What, for a while, told you you knew her well,
What live cry for her survives in your thought,

Who she was for you, what she meant, feared, thought.
She had trunks, jammed with what her love judged good;
Are they still somewhere, tagged & indexed well,
Or are they like my pictures of her lost?
I've saved what she left—stale or fragile now—
Latin books, laughs, wine, lists of what to do.

Should you have questions, do feel free to ask,
Given the always present tense of thought.
Though I know no time is as bad as now,
Recall her you—I could!—let him make good
The tale of that naked pure young fool, lost
Before I got a chance to know her well.

I should say, as well: beyond what I ask
Lies the you you lost, alive: in my thought
Still planning to be good. Redeem him now.

Now ask your thought for this lost good. Farewell.

UNABASHED

Unabashed
as some landscapes are
(a lakeshape, say,
lying and lifting
under a cupping sky)
     so angels are,
entire with each other,
their wonderful bodies
obedient, their strengths
interchanging—
     or so
we imagine them
hoping
by saying these things of them
to invent human love.

AS IS

Objects new to this place, I receive you.
It was I who sent for each of you.
The house of my mother is empty.
I have emptied it of all her things.
The house of my mother is sold with
All its trees and their usual tall music.
I have sold it to the stranger,
The architect with three young children.

Things of the house of my mother,
You are many. My house is
Poor compared to yours and hers.
My poor house welcomes you.
Come to rest here. Be at home. Please
Do not be frantic do not
Fly whistling up out of your places.
You, floor- and wall-coverings, be
Faithful in flatness; lie still;
Try. By light or by dark
There is no going back.
You, crystal bowls, electrical appliances,
Velvet chair and walnut chair,
You know your uses; I wish you well.
My mother instructed me in your behalf.
I have made room for you. Most of you
Knew me as a child; you can tell
We need not be afraid of each other.

And you, old hopes of the house of my mother,
Farewell.

LATE

FOR MARIE CANDEE BIRMINGHAM, MY MOTHER

I

Dark on a bright day, fear of you is two-poled,
Longing its opposite. Who were we?
What for? dreaming, I haunt you unconsoled.

Rewarded as I force thought outward, I see
A warbler, a Myrtle, marked by coin-gold—
I feel lucky, as if I'd passed a test,
And try my luck, to face the misery
Of loss on loss, find us, and give us rest.
Once we birdwatched, eyeing shrub & tree
For the luck beyond words that was our quest;
Your rings flashing, you showed me day-holed
Owls, marsh blackbirds on red wings, the crest
Kingfishers bear. Mother, dreams are too cold
To eye the dark woodland of your bequest.

2

To eye the dark woodland of your bequest
I wear the fire of diamond on my hand,
Flawed extravagance of your first love expressed
In a many-faceted engagement band.
Recklessly cut with the blaze I invest
In my dazzling flaws, careless of weight,
The fiery cast of mind that I love planned
To sacrifice carat-points for this bright state.
It is yours still, and I go talismanned
By you to find you, though I'm lost & late.
You left this for me; ringed I go dressed

To mother us, mother, to isolate
And name the flight of what, mouth to rich breast,
We meant while we were together to create.

3

We meant while we were together to create
A larger permanence, as lovers do,
Of perfecting selves: I would imitate
By my perfections, yours; I would love you
As you me, each to the other a gate
Opening on intimate gardens and
Amiable there. Mother you were new
At it but when you looped us in the bands
Of clover hope to be each other's due,
The hope at least lasted; here I still stand
Full of the verb you had to predicate.
Though you as subject now are contraband
Half hidden, half disguised to intimidate,
I recognize your diamond on my hand.

4

I recognize your diamond on my hand
As the imagined world where we were whole.
Now among boxed boxes, pine roots, & Queens sand,
You have changed places with this bit of coal,
Dark to light, light to dark. To understand
The dark your child never was afraid of
I go lightless sightless birdless mole
In the dark which is half what words are made of;
I enter the dark poems memories control,
Their dark love efficient under day love.

Down I go down through the oldest unscanned
Scapes of mind to skim the dim parade
Of images long neglected lost or banned,
To root for the you I have not betrayed.

5

To root for the you I have not betrayed
I hunt the ovenbird we never found—
Or guessed we'd found when something leafbrown strayed
Under the trees where soft leaves lay year round.
When you'd said, "Hush," and we'd obeyed (obeyed
Lifelong too long) "Tea/cher!" we heard; the shy
Bird spoke itself, "Tea/cher!" from the dim ground
The call came plain enough to recognize
And we went out following the sound.
It went before us in the dusk; its cries
Go before me now, swerve & dip in shade
Woman daughter bird teacher teach me. Skies
Boughs brush tufts; blind I have lost where we played
All trust in love, to the dark of your disguise.

6

Trust in love lost to the dark of your disguise,
I forget if I loved you; I forget
If, when I failed, you requisitioned lies;
Did we make believe we saw the bird, and set
On my lifelong list what my long life denies:
That we found what we wanted side by side?

But I did see you bird I see you yet
Your live glance glinting from leafdust; you hide

Calling, colorless, your brief alphabet
Sharp. Wait, wait for me. Flash past, dusty bride,
Stand safe, rosefooted, before my finite eyes.
Sing, undeafen me. Bird be identified.
Speak yourself. I dread love that mystifies.
Say we wanted what we found side by side.

7

I say I wanted what I found at your side.
("Is that your mother?" yes. "But she's a tea/
cher." Yes. I see that.) Reading, sunned, outside,
I see your lit hand on the page, spirea
Shaking light on us; from your ring I see slide
A sun, showering its planets across skies
Of words making, as you read or I or we,
A cosmos, ours. Its permanence still defies
The dark, in sparkles on this page; fiery,
It makes its statement clear: light multiplies.
No matter on whose flawed hand what jewel rides
Or who quickens to what bird with jeweled eyes,
The light of the planet is amplified.
Bird your life is diamond and amplifies.

Replay

The luck beyond birds that was our quest
I find in you. Although I'm lost & late
Our hope at least lasted; here I still stand
In your dark love, efficient under day love;
It goes before me in the dark, its cries
Sharp. Wait, wait for me. Flash past, dusty bride.
Make your statement clear: light multiplies.

OF CERTAIN STUDENTS

Once, teachers were giants of the numinous
—Plato, Plotinus, Porphyry, Iamblichus—
Whose sandaled academies trod holily on air;
I praise them but (in class) am not envious.
Ritual can't spin up out of the likes of us;
We're safe.
       Yet we, not even friends, do exchange
Fierce energies. Playing at change,
We do change. Sometimes, you gesture and
From off your hands blades of light flash.

Sometimes in your absences
I turn you into lists of things
To do, and do them.

Often in your presences
I make lists, in the thinlooped snares
That language casts, of things I ought to say
(And you could sing them)
Great things—and some days your tongues
Are so quick they spring them.

FOR A SEASON

We saw we had few words to exchange when two by two
By two over our heads birds like omens flew
Making space between us dangerous.

Glances can be truthful; this I learned
When with your sharp breath the time turned
Very sharp and felicitous.

And truth is unknowable. Who knows
How far to where the loving goes
When its action makes free of us?

Generously we lay together
Under the Irish weather.
It was summer due to us.

LULLABY

Sleep now, hush my
fragile beast,
fed new child, sleep.
Look at you, soft,
life locked to you
safe in your fist;
no light enters yet
like flowers you retain
all the light there is
blotted up like a stain.
Even at dusk you lie,
though this room looks east,
luminous in it; the shadows
stoop so you are centered
as you leach from the air
the last of the light
to show you as holy
as you are fair.
Sleep now. There there.
Good night.

A THIRD THANK-YOU LETTER

for the gift of the Vert-Galant

The Seine and the sky refract each other's rain.

Unrefracting, I
lost June looking for you.

Every river needs an island
to underline its wetness with
that surge of green plume
every island needs.

And here, among the green where
the curve of the river ramparts retains
the river in stone, and the curves in pencil
retain the pulse of these words,
you are.

It is after all late spring: I write
"You are here, after all."
For the rest of the morning
I do not need to remember
anything; for the rest of the day
there is the morning to remember;
I think we remember it together.

The blunt barge nose slowly shows
the middle bridge arch has been chosen, and
glides under; behind
the long flat of it, the person with
bright mind in the less bright white
wheelhouse looks down over coal-

heaps at Vert-Galant, glances with
your brightness,
waves and grins
above the integrating water.

In the July mist I welcome you.

You offer me the river, grey
as the sky but glaucous like Homer and
olive leaves or like puddles of oil paint
cupping dark green & pulsing silver
in every direction.

Babbling, I've missed you.
In St.-Séverin I did not see the pillar I
talked about though it leapt up like
you for us, living, the line emerging
from the stone in three dimensions yet
linear therefore envisioned and springing
clear as mind from living brain.
I am in fact usually
much too busy to look for you.
No wonder I catch cold. The casual
river does better, always watching the sky.

Opposite, along the outer thigh of the given river,
some trees are missing from the row, plane trees
gone to lighten traffic where the toy
cars speed toward Notre-Dame (you
are, in them, less reflected than you are,
my brightness, by the river
though their metal winks for you boldly). Today

the river is what you have given me,
and the locust the willows the chestnut
of the small in-position park, emerging head-down

from the river's undulant pelvic floor,
lying along the modular inner thighs of the river
new green to encourage the signals
of new lovers, games of new children, new
farewells of old voyagers.
                    Because I have been here
watching and in place for one hour
you have come flooding back to me
bearing ransom. Awash with that limpid
identity, I take you in. All islands are
always being born; each needs
a like inhabitant, interacting, riverborne:
here I am, just down from the palace of justice
greening, crowning, new at the feet of Notre-Dame,
assuming your welcome
and welcoming you
gratefully

grown to want
what I have
and to have
what I want
where I want
what I have
to be

DISCOVERY

Though I sit here alone I
am smiling and
realize why as I find
that the answer (to my own
old poser of who will be
my magna mater) is clear;
I can even understand
her invisibility
for she, the grand
mother (I've always needed)
    is surely here
     too close to see
     for I am she.
Laughing she explains nothing.

My life is given back to me.

For we survived seedtime
(some seeds pop their pods and jump away;
some cased out of clumps by gold birds
float off, alight, and again drift;
some, deer after drinking drop
near a pleasant stream) we
survived and the winter
was kind to the seed
and now the winter has lifted;
I leave the season of need.

Daughter gone to lover of daughter,
sons to lovers of sons, all

have gone from me readily
with the extended almost soundless leap
of trust in genital clemency.
Left to myself I discover
that what had to spring together
has sprung together and the fields
are beds of blossoming,
the hollow meadows fill
again with blossoming.

Blessing the gardeners I do not doubt
the benefits the blessing yields
as daily less anxiously
I walk out among them
or windsoft beyond them
unheard unheeded
not lost not needed
reaching invisibly
for what is great yet proper to me
and cannot but mother me:
unconsidered liberty.

ADVICE:
Ad Haereditates (1)

The water:
    I pour it
    with care
into these seven jars for
you seven,
sacred voyagers
soon to be launched.
    One of you will
one day need it;
I have seen signs
    in your faces; one
    will need it.
Each of you is
I judge able to need it.

I pray this good water
be to your hand in time of want.

I look into your faces o
my God my children!
    (yes, such talk, the least-
    considered catch of the heart,
    makes pagans guess false worship.
    Well, not their fault; they do not
    know there is one difference
    language does not make.)

You suppose, my seven, that you too
are pagan, my lovely children. When

your turn calls, you will
       lose the lift of doubt.

You are setting out now.
I may not be here when you
      come back. Two or three
may find me still around
or find me elsewhere,
on the road or in
grandbabies' faces; sooner or later
however, we meet again.

You have a taste of the water,
    coronal, in the small
    vials you always carry.
In case you need it, in case
you've half forgotten the true
flavor when someone wants to
sell you lots of wetness
and you need something sustaining,
    or in case
dreaming you dream you are no longer
refreshed by thinking of drinking it—
well, my children, in any such
great emergency
    go ahead,
    break the vial open,
drink your drop, you
won't be able to forget the flavor, then.
Being grown up, having
chosen it and tasted it again,
you may ache
for all—yourself too—who are
usually thirsty but
you won't be unsure of it;

no one ever is, or has been in my
time or my mother's either.

For there is never as much water
available to share or store as we'd like,
never. Nor do most of us manage
to give enough time to locating
new springs and keeping
old sorts of jars, vials, bottles
both safe and accessible. I hear
they do it better, in some places
nowadays; they have special processes.
Probably, voyaging, you'll learn
improvements in methods I haven't
dreamed of. That's progress. For instance,
one way my mother didn't know, I learned
on a voyage of my own: Be dry be as dry
with yourself as you can, so as to
absorb what you need in passing
from the ground or right from the air.
It can happen. Though you miss
the shocking joy of taste,
it will do you its good anyway.

Now, I must say that I have not
tried hard enough, left you enough
except for emergencies, even in quantity. That's
not the worst though: I haven't foreseen
every emergency. There too
I did not do as well as I was able.
            But you will forgive me,
those of you anyway who never face
emergency I failed to foresee.
            The one who does meet it
head-on will not forgive me

unless
maybe
after.
When you separate, try
to remember to say
(at least! to yourself)
some little
ceremonious
good-by;
take leave
of each other
gracefully.
It saves agony later
when you meet again.
The old ceremony,
the effort you gave it, will
stir your memory warmly,
children.

I've often heard,
"The greater the quantity
the less the thirst in & around you,"
therefore these jars—though
I believe those who say
one drop can suffice
for a lifetime, and no lifetime
lacks that drop. Some disagree;
you'll see for yourselves.

What we know for certain
is that this is water
—mine to give you
what I may of it—
that nothing
can spoil.

GLIDING

A.M., Town Garden

Sometimes, riding the thermals, the swallows
drift backwards a little at their ease
before they tilt, slide forward down,
and drive their blades of wings stroke on stroke
to catch another column of wind; it lifts
them and they soar. It's a spinning soaring
in the morning windchange; tight
spirals take them to such heights they
vanish; viewed ecstatic, edge-on at their
curve into sheer sky, they turn as
invisible as the principles of flight
              all this time crying
              short crying
—the i's and e's of excellent action—
to say their only
effort is the effort of the act:
sounds we have all sometimes needed,
never made, and seldom deserved
to have a hearer hear.
I look up at them from shade in a walled
well of green among roses and boxwood.
To practice is to take a chance on joy, I think;
the one use of what they do is skill; skill
works against limits to cancel out
sloppiness, tedium, and some pain;
one skill is plenty; taken to the full
is morning swallow-soaring, easily

voicing the sounds of inner
rejoicing in its readiness.

P.M., Mountain Flight Terrain

To look out from high places without flinching
(I do it belly to the ground) is to suspect how speech
might work, were we ready to face
the drop
into our inner space and find for mind
however awkwardly words and syntax
to negotiate aloud what otherwise
is mystery. It is to suspect our
gravity would change could we surface
the words of that integrating music
we all hear privately.

Hang-gliders haul their gear up here.
They've worked for years to manage a freedom.
They sleep under schema of da Vinci drawings,
keep calculators, wind-tables, equipment catalogues
in the bedside table drawer.
They have passion, brag, argue, share
their dozens of small implements of skill,
their geometry, costumes, support
facilities; train like acrobats,
measure up to standards; are licensed,
play. Clumsy, thick-boned,
beautiful, they practice doing
what they are not suited to;
a second of horror
collects their massy bags of flesh dense
with life and throws them out over
8,000 feet of moving air, as they aim to catch
with the fabric of their thought-up wings their

sustenance. They take flight: people
sail among eagles, as alert,
electric, spending as the mad.
They change the axioms, until
after short soaring,
they home in on a managed
flat of mowed green ground. Sometimes
they can walk back up whole mountains
to their cars, imagining
the next leap into longer independent flight.

Though they'd seem to need wings not hands
to endure the insubstantial field,
having made wings by hand,
they face it readily. It is so huge
it solicits the delight
of those who live open-armed; they
afford it; they enter its emptiness
in a posture of embrace.
Their point of view
would torment others, the hungry,
the cramped and landless, the sad,
who would look through the fields of joy at
the thousand horizontal miles of growing ground
whose juices might, in season,
alleviate their ancient needs.
I'm the ordinary middle of these extremes.

My skill is small and local;
like many ordinary people
I scan the closer mystery: thinking
we want the skill to press against
the limits of our speech, we rehearse
the accents of the inner world, tuneful but
invisible, in hopes the outer ear
will quicken to thought spoken

until
            across the empty air
of personal separateness—and all
are separate—we will sound true or
human to each other,
human kind,
hearing, heard, and
recognized. We elect
readiness to practice this.

Straight ahead of me is sky.
It is wholly flourishing. Below it & me
the earth in its rock-fold distances
is starred by geodes of inhabited villages
where cliff & gorge divert the wind.
Three hundred years ago they snaked a crazy
carriage road over this maritime Alp
just below these heights. Once a woman
kept an inn on it, and help for horses.

The air is ripe. My fists unclench,
and the air, filled with the odor of
thyme & lavender I lie on, fills my hands.
Unshaken by my readiness
or the smallness of my readiness
—or my ignorance of how
the hollows in our speech will fill
as we rehearse aloud against our limits
the names and principled tunes for shapes
and fragrances and absences of shapes
we have in mind—
I envision the next leap, the next
thousand years of practice,
the eventual skill
become like independent flight, habitual.

THE GREAT DEAD,
WHY NOT, MAY KNOW

FOR JOAN PAUL

No grief goes unrelieved;
some days, half meaning to,
I turn my undefended back
on the grey & snarling scene
of my dissociating pack
and hope.

Some suppose that this post-natal life
where all we have is time, is fetal life,
is where as we bounce and flex in time
our years of moons change us
into beings viable not here
but somewhere attentive. Suppose,
borne down on, we are birthed
into a universe where love's not crazy;
and that split out of time is
death into a medium where
love is the element we cry out to breathe,
big love, general as air here,
specific as breath.

I want to talk to those outlanders
whose perspective I admire;
I listen often to the voices of the dead, and
it feels like my turn in the conversation.
I want to ask, say, Yeats (or
someone else it would make sense to,
Crashaw, Blake, H.D. who
worked out Sappho's honey simile,

Joan word-lover you too, all you
who know what English has to do
with a possible answer)

And I'd say, to set up the question:
Listen,
after over a hundred lifetimes
of summers of honey since Sappho's,
of beekeepers (who set out orchard
rows of nectarplants to bloom
before and after the appletrees,
      who sow alfalfa or tupelo,
      clover or roses,
      "all roses," all summer,
then break the combs out of their dark
and decant the honey heavy & flowery)
—listen, it's no different.
Honey's still dangerous.
Honey's pervasive.
Hunger for honey scalds if satisfied.
I know; I walk around dry-lipped;
my throat burns, and the August air at noon
ices it as I breathe because
I've been eating honey right from the spoon

and (as you, outside observers, can recall)
though petal & pollen nod golden & mild,
honey here burns like gall
and, having burned bitter
      sweet   raw   hot
generates a language for wild
love not limited to pollensoft
couplings of lovers; it generates
the longing to use that language
though there be not any one

to speak it to. Such honey
expressed as if it must be as love
which colors all encounters and lasts
long after one love has gone to seed,
changes the throat of a speaker
till it aches with expectancy
as it asks:

WHAT (as at last I ask
        you of the outland honeyed universe,
        you great dead)
what do you do with love
when it is no more sexual
        than I am sexual,
when it is general
—in me, not mine—
and yet shapes the air,
like breath, like a honeyed
breath of air carrying
meaning between
me and everything there is;
when as if it must it defies
my daily exercise of savagery
and cause for guilt;
when it is absolute,
too sudden to disguise,
unmapped,
unlocalized,
stubbornly addressed
to any eyes—
though it find me no less slothful nor
in any way more kind or wise?

What but
(since the love is in the language)

call it hope
—that helps a little—
and hope to imitate your inlands of example
by praising the possible;
what then but praise the ripening
cure of language which plays
among questions and answers
mediating even love and grief,
what but
       —as the window the morning
      as the foot the tilt of the ground
      as the river the lights of its city—
praise how the actions of language or honey
seem in their transport to express,
from the collected heat and sweetness
of hearing and speaking,
           something
smaller and more human than belief,
some reason to read these thick omens
as good and those outlands as relief.

From *The Green Dark*, 1988

ON A LIBRARY OF CONGRESS PHOTO
OF EUNICE B. WINKLESS, 1904

Eunice, flexible flyer of summer, rides
across the noon fair
short-stirruped astride
her tall white mare,
her power implied
loosely in a practiced grip.
Her life is in her hands;
her living found, she lets nothing slip.

The pool glints like a tame star on the ground.
The ramp up the two-story tower, if
ramshackle, is ready.
Martial music starts.
Here she comes bareback. Having hitched
her triple-flounced Gibson-girl arts lightly
about her, her hands rein calm in.

Regal as Iphigenia
taking the upward course
in a drift of white eyelet muslin
she rides the animal horse.
Merrily fife & drum pace
their climb. Women think prayers,
set to not-look, just in case.
Men do not snigger, forget
their faces/ladies/bets, and stare
once she reaches the platform.
Music quits her exalted there.
Sounds, gathered to silence, swarm

stormhead about her stance. This crowd, knowing
horses, wonders if the big mare
shudders as it holds still. The pool shows
flatness: no wind. That's good. A brittle
drumroll rains. The drumsticks stop.
She leans to the mare's neck, smiling a little.

Out & groundless horse & girl drop
flying clear of equilibrium
Her body jockeying air
touches only bridle & with one
knee, horse, as nothing to spare
they head for the hope they head
in dread in dread for the pool.

To herself she says among her wet hair,
"Did it again. Damn fool."

I need her dreadful ease, its immense self-reference.
I watch to catch her hand-span skill address
the radius of her practice then guess,
self-tested, at its circumference.

Yet since I made all this up from one snapshot
it is fictive ink, not history.
What I think of her may be ready or not
to be telling. Who can make sense?

And, when do I act on better evidence?

THE PROBLEM OF FREEDOM & COMMITMENT

(She is 6 years old.)

In her first dot-to-dot book of puzzles
the last one left undone looks too hard.
It has hundreds of numbers. She prefers
the two-digit ones that trace out as
big-headed animals with big eyes
but she decides to give this one a try.
Soon she has a notion of one part of how
the picture will turn out to be.
She doesn't like it. Not one bit. She sees
it may be more trouble than it's worth so she goes
slower, hunting for the next consecutive
numbers, no longer anxious to find them
but anxious once they're found, fixed on,
and another strand of line goes down.
"It's too much. It's all mixed up," she thinks.
"Even the good parts are scribbly. There are
millions of books like this, all different;
I could just leave this mess and get
a new book, with no horrors in it,
a nice one, that I'd like." But she goes on
absent minded, thinking *picture,* working out
the one she's started, worse and worse.
Right now there's nothing else to do, and if, she thinks,
she's false to this the first unpleasant one,
which is so complex her predictions are guesses,
which could be the most important one in the book,
maybe the puzzle will make her take a second look
and nothing she starts on will ever get done.

THE PROBLEM OF FICTION

(She is 13 years old.)

She always writes poems. This summer
she's starting a novel. It's in trouble already.
The characters are easy—a girl
and her friend who is a girl
and the boy down the block with his first car,
an older boy, sixteen, who sometimes
these warm evenings leaves his house to go dancing
in dressy clothes though it's still light out.
The girl has a brother who has lots of friends,
is good in math, and just plain good which
doesn't help the story. The story
should have rescues & escapes in it
which means who's the bad guy; he couldn't be
the brother or the grandpa or the father either,
or even the boy down the block with his first car.
People in novels have to need something,
she thinks, that it takes about
two hundred pages to get.
She can't imagine that. Nothing
she needs can be got; if it could
she'd go get it: the answer to nightmares;
a mother who'd be proud of her; doing things
a mother could be proud of; having hips
& knowing how to squeal at the beach laughing
when the boy down the block picked her up & carried her
& threw her in the water. If she'd laughed
squealing he might still take her swimming
& his mother wouldn't say she's crazy, she would
not have got her teeth into his shoulder till

well yes she bit him, and the marks
lasted & lasted, his mother said so,
but that couldn't be in a novel.

She'll never squeal laughing, she'd never
not bite him, she hates cute girls, she hates
boys who like them. Biting is embarrassing
and wrong & she has no intention of doing it again
but she would if he did if he dared,
and there's no story if there's no hope of change.

THE PROBLEM OF GRATIFIED DESIRE

(She is 15 years old.)

If she puts honey in her tea
and praises prudence in the stirring up
she drinks, finally,
a drop of perfect sweetness
hot at the bottom of the cup.

There will be
pleasures more complex than it
(pleasure exchanged were infinite)
but none so cheap
more neat or definite.

THE PROBLEM OF LOVING-KINDNESS

(She is 17 years old.)

She has gone soft
her body suddenly
lovely to her.
Gratefully
she wants to speak & be
believed, to see
his eyes darken with quiet & deepen
learning they agree.
But he believes as if deaf
what he says—
words for shocks of love that sound like
invincible grabs snatches whams hits, like
Cuchulain's *tae bolga*—a weapon that striking
her anywhere would shoot, in an electric
flex of tentacles, need of him
through every member, follicle
of hair, & finger-end—its thousand hooks pointed
so backward & sharp they must be endured
because to remove them would eviscerate.
She has to turn down his talk. She says
if love struck her like that she'd refuse.
If crazed endurance were the only ecstasy
she'd opt for evisceration on the spot.
She feels flat-footed, he's so carried away.
Since he's not listening she's silent;
she eats the rest of what she has to say,
her dreadful dowdy words,
the kind he won't hear,
full of dumb feeling,
"My darling. My dear."

WEARING THE GAZE OF AN ARCHAIC STATUE

The juggler in her suit of nerve
is eyes and hands. The rest of her
dangles soft-shoe below her shoulders,
relaxed, co-operating. She knows
that to toss things out is something
but not much, not important; is
for the sake of when, picturing
a ribboning like water spurting,
she is holding nothing.
She is on her own here;
she is not just letting go,
and her small touching skill is:
holding nothing.

Holding on, she is not a juggler.
She is you and me, hands full of things
she must practice juggling to get out from under.
She sets her feet and begins.
She smiles like Pomona, offering
three, a dozen, lifeless, bits & pieces she
can't get rid of; she presents them as
shapeliness and they lose weight.
The rhythm clarifies something, maybe her.
She settles back, a laughing fountain
pumping particles.
The order of motion emerges.
Up they loft one by one, she is tossing,
up, spheres, sticks, boxes, soft, metallic,
out with them she goes till her hands

close on nothing, are just
touched for the electric
seconds of netting the elements
with energy in air.
They drop, sprout, up, out, drop, up, & slowly
each touch makes her invisible save as
a phase of the great legislation
she proposes to obey.

"LOVE IS NOT LOVE"

FOR ELENA CORNARO, FIRST WOMAN PH.D., BORN IN PADUA, 1647;
AND FOR THOSE WHOSE CHILDREN ARE IN PAIN HERE AND NOW

It is cold. I am
drawing my life around me to get warm.
Holes in the blanket can't be re-woven.
Some thorns caught in it still scratch. Some tear.

I reach for comfort
to the left-out lives of women here and gone.
They lend them willingly. They know my need.
They do not hate me for crying. It beats despair.

Elena Cornaro
hands me her cinderella cap & gown.
I put them on. Stiff fur. But intact: she
(when eleven! just in time) saw

in a flash the mortal needles
their rain of cupidity
aimed at eyes across the looking air,

laughed and in singleness averted them
shielded by choice against the dark & steel.
She stopped herself in herself, refined
her will, and brought her mind virgin to bear

stretched across nine languages—nine sun-
keepers, their word-clusters grapes
of intellect, for wine
she pours me now.

It stings like speed:
Ph.D., TB, breath on fire, young,
she sported her doctoral vair
in vain. She too died of blood.
Yet the mind she trained
had warmed her in the storm
(all storms one storm) where
she'd left no hostage howling to be freed,
no captive mouths to feed;
in her sight, no punctual winter swarm
of guilt—pale bees whose attack breeds
paralysis, and dread of snow
that masks the snare.
I am stuck in cold. It is deaf. It is eiron.

What has happened to my child
is worse than I can tell you
and I'm ashamed to say
is more than I can bear.

Elena, listen.
My body speaks nine languages but the greed
of me is stuck, my exposed eyes prickle,
I think blank, he's lost out there, I'm scared.

What I have borne, I bear.

Oh I praise your continence, kind life, pure form.
Your way's one way, not mine; you're summer-stopped;
my meadow's mud, turned stone in this icy air.

Whose fault is it? It's at the root my fault.
But in your cape, I come to?
And I'm in your care?
As he is mine, so I am yours to bear

alive. He is still alive. He has not died of it.
Wronged. Wrong.

Regardless love is hard to bear.
It has no hospital.
It is its own fireplace.
All it takes is care.

Well, when you grew intimate with pain,
what did you do. How did you do it. Where.
That, this? Thanks. Suppose I'm not in time.
Is it worth a try. I'll try,

try to conceive of room to spare,
a surround of walls steady and steadying
an uncracked ceiling & a quiet floor,
a morning room, a still room
where we'd bring mind to bear upon
our consequences—we who make
no difference, who ignoring
absence of response have chosen
ways to love we can't go back on
and we won't,

regardless:
like your holy aura, Elena,
like your singleness, my fertility,
your tiny eminence, your early death;

like our Vassar Miller, her persistent listening;
like our Tillie Olsen, her persistent flowering;
like our Djuna and our Emily
their insolent beauty visored,
disguised as hermit crabs;
like our Sarah Jewett's faithful gaze—

cast down—
like my long-drawn-out mistakes.

Elena maybe we
remember each other as room
for when to cry, what to cry for,
cry to whom.

HANGZHOU, LAKE OF THE POETS

FOR JOE AND HEATHER CUOMO

Morning

Reading the bones, wetting a fingertip
to trace archaic characters, I feel
a breeze of silence flow up past my wrist,
icy. Can I speak here? The bones say I must.
As the first light strikes across the lake, magpies
scream, and the cast bones say the work must come true,
it's been true all along, we are what we do
out on our digs. Dictor and looker, all eyes,
with spade and a jeweler's loupe I sift mud & dust
for bone, for shellcast. Spy, archeologist
of freshness, I expect sight-made-sound to reveal
fear cold at the throat of change, and loosen its grip
so that mind, riding the bloodwarm stream, wells up
as the speech that bears it and is telling.

Evening

Magpies scream. Though the tongues of birds
say Now and warn forward, free of a live past,
we seek back and forth for change, the ghostly sparkling
of our watertable under everywhere.
If I don't speak to tap & ease it out,
I go dry & dumb & will die wicked.
On the lake of the poets a stone lamp flickers.
It casts eight moons dancing, casting doubt
on the moon that rides above the winter air.

Ice thaws in a poet's throat; the springing
truth is fresh. It wakes taste. The taste lasts.
Language floods the mud; mind makes a cast of words;
it precipitates, mercurial, like T'ang discourse
riding the tidal constant of its source.

LEVELS

A stone fence holds the heat.
Close to it, the earth face opens:
a little eye
rimmed with dirt crumbs;
a nerve inside winks
alive with ants.
The yellow-shafted flicker
before it strikes inspects
the spot, drops
from the fence, calculates,
lifts the lid off.
Air fractures, and
inner alleys collapse, as
diamond-cutter the flicker
like a good writer starts
at the heart.
Its bill its tool,
it chisels toward the fault,
beaks at the crux of it, and
chambers of egg-cases
crack open. As the bird
eats, insects by hundreds
scatter in patterns carrying
clustered eggs, rushing
some to safety, later.

Ants leave me cold,
their bitty parts reflexive,
like cells of lung or muscle,

unprincipled, lacking
a visible body to serve—
oh, why qualify. Ant-mystery
drifts out of mind.
The bird is flicker;
its action exhibits it,
pinioned to a wheel which
the mind's eye axles,
the mind's eye spins.

THE ROYAL GATE

Little Jacqueline Pascal played with Blaise
re-inventing Euclid (Papa told them to).
While he made up conic sections, she wrote plays
& got papa out of jail when Richelieu
liked her long impromptu poem in his praise.
I haven't read her verse. It's not in print.
Blaise invented: the wristwatch, a kind
of computer, fluid mechanics, the hint
for digital calques, probabilities,
the syringe, space as vacuum, the claims of lay
theologians. He thought (he thought) at his ease.

In her convent Jacqueline kept the rules.
On or under every desert there are pools.

OUTSIDE THE FERTILE CRESCENT

Too long out of her seashell, too far away
from green waves sparkling as they lick the sky,
Aphrodite falters. Shallow ponds delay
her sea-search. Off course, inland, tired, dry,
she takes a man's words seriously
when he offers water. He owns a well.
She settles in his oasis. His one tree,
his human heart, cast their spell;
for such implosion she serves him gratefully.
He keeps her safe from his city of those
who are wicked. She gets water enough,
cupfuls, pitcherfuls, to cook & wash clothes,
not to plunge in. Pillared when she calls his bluff,
at dawn her salt crystals gleam, flushed with rose.

SYNTHESIS

Elemental as weather this love
is of delicate appetite.

Leaves must reflect to the air
the surfeit of light they eat.

You are tender as lettuce;
your mineral bitterness is
suspended in sweet water,
my health in its element.

DE-FUSING THE USUAL CRIMINAL METAPHORS

Pity the idle who (though daily our lives
must make room for those who use clubs guns knives)
speak as if a penis were, when erect,
a tower of hard. The dear part we inspect
is always quick to shrink from violence;
hand-small, it fits any woman well.
Jocktalk of huge dongs grown trenchant as they swell
stands in, to hide the gathered evidence
of our true brute force; it is greed, not sex,
that we secrete & feed, till it infects
the whole life not the part with rape-like impotence.

The part comes on hopeful, nudging, nuzzling, tip
bent damp and rosy toward a soft eclipse.
Here's no jackhammer jammed home ruthlessly
but the yielding press of stamen under bee,
glowing at the sweetness of us; neatly met
and heedful (clumsy) as we sweat.
Here's no plow, ramrod, sword; no piercing cut—
if root, tender, a root-bud, just unshut;
though worm a word of yes and asking blessing,
though hole a blessing asking mouth of yes,
as one soft-tissued muscle noses plumply through
other muscles, their lax loop drawn. Here, we two
make touch our second sight as, no longer blind,
we each bring a self—big bones, guts, thoughts, hearts—
to local focus, trusting the ease we find
beyond discovery of our nervous secret parts
(as if hot trust might disinfect our minds

and its oils ease the human kind in us
to be in public as in private generous
with exchanges larger than the ease we're thinking of;
as if what we have to make in making love is love).

JAMAICA WILDLIFE CENTER, QUEENS, NEW YORK

On a south wind the sea air off
the flats and inlets of Jamaica Bay
mirrors as they do,
almost wavelessly, space recast as
flatness, long
diminishings of blue
borne lightly in toward
earth colors, steel-lit ochres,
rose-mucky brown, greens.

I am a window that takes this in
like a door, or mouth.
I spit nothing out.
I wait—like the egrets,
egrets spread on distant trees
like a wash of table-linen
for the sun to dry.

Were I a room I'd be stuffed
but what windows admit
I transfigure
to the bite-sized images
intelligence eats & eats
eagerly.

Splotches of white
contract, lift
into springing figures; bird.
One by one, one is a leader, up

off the green dark
they go into sun.
They are coming this way
to lunch in the shallows.
I too am good at hunger;
it never deserts me.
I admit as I am able
frank delight
in the deaths and decisions
of visible appetite.
Deep delight;
it is for—not of—myself,
it is for you
I write
of the storage and freshness
of keepers
of the life
of appetite.

THE IDES OF MAY

(FOR MY CHILDREN ENTERING PARENTHOOD)

Every seventh second the wood thrush
speaks its loose curve until in ten minutes
the thicket it lives in is bounded
by the brand of its sound.

Every twenty-eight days the leisurely
moon diagrams the light way, east to west,
to describe mathematics and keep us unstuck
on our arched ground.

Every generation the child hurries out of childhood head bared to the face-making blaze
of bliss and distress, giving a stranger power to
enter, wound, astound.

BETWEEN

FOR MY DAUGHTER

Composed in a shine of laughing, Monique brings in sacks
of groceries, unloads them, straightens, and stretches her back.

The child was a girl, the girl is a woman; the shift
is subtle and absolute, worn like a gift.

The woman, once girl once child, now is deft in her ease,
is door to the forum, is cutter of keys.

In space that her torque and lift have prefigured and set free
between her mother and her child the woman stands
having emptied her hands.

HARD-SHELL CLAMS

When it was too late for him to provide
his own share in my happy childhood, my
father stopped clowning out stories & tried
for a whole day to see me—a good try
by both of us. Back we went to the seaside
of old summers, we two, we talked, we swam,
sleek with cocoa butter that caught the sand—
a glitter like chain mail guarding who I am
from his used blue gaze that stared to understand.
Closed, stuck closed, I watched us—far me far him—
go small, smaller, further, father, joy dim
in beach light. Our last chance, last perfect day.

We laughed. We ate four dozen hard-shell clams.
We swallowed what I would not let us say.

OUT OF EDEN

Under the May rain over the dug grave
my mother is given canticles and I who believe
in everything watch flowers stiffen to new bloom.

Behind us the rented car fabricates a cave.
My mother nods: Is he? He is. But, is? Nods.
Angels shoo witches from this American tomb.

The nod teaches me. It is something I can save.
He left days ago. We, so that we too may leave,
install his old belongings in a bizarre new room.
I want to kneel indignantly anywhere and rave.

    Well, God help us, now my father's will is God's.
    At games and naming he beat Adam. He loved his Eve.
    I knew him and his wicked tongue. What he had, he
                          gave.

I do not know where to go to do it, but I grieve.

PATIENT

The woman sleeps, old hand under old cheek,
skin like white iris crumpled, baby-sweet.
She'd let herself go but she's too weak
to organize admission of defeat.
Morning. Her girl tries to get her to speak
but she's too busy with plans to protect
the one thing she doesn't dare lose, her own,
her married name, "i," not "e," that's correct,
not her first name, her whole name, hers alone
(first names can be anybody's). Some days
she can't say it so she writes it. They
steal her name. Eyes shut, she stares at warm haze.
Then she smiles as she remembers to pray:
Trust. Someone to talk to. Something to say.

MUSEUM OUT OF MIND

Whatever it was I used to call you out loud
when I was twenty, ten, or less, I forget. Odd—
I shy from recalling the syllables of how

the golden age once spoke (say, as we talked non-stop
after school, or having our hair done, or as you
chose green peas pod by pod while I watched you shop).

Later, myself mother, I called you the motherdear
no child of mine would use—but one of the baby
humwords must have come first. And I am infant here

before your advanced degrees in death, seeking speech
in words of a tongue I am spelling out of you who could,
by the stars and letters of a map you'd make, teach

(Queens Hermes, alphabet giver) anyone to find
the essential simple, and to translate all
locations into constellations of the mind.

I talk to your absence. Daft. Grotesque. I begin
to see you as grotesque, yes a joke, a guess,
a grotesque of the grave I wept to leave you in.

Birds love dead trees. They like to strip a shred of bark,
tug at it, shake it, lunch on egg-case and insect,
and I go after you like that. Graves are

grounded in the mind though the cemetery keeps
grounds & groundplan, their care perpetual; yours is
in the sad best section, comical—we Stoics

are all comics—among Mafia and their daily,
like you, communicant women. A solitary,
motherdear, you loved the look of community

as, dogged in practice, you believed undaunted
and behaved, relentlessly, as you believed,
so that at times your present company haunts me

like a storm of comic joy. Into the eight-body
plot grandma bought and put grandpa at the bottom,
she went next old raceme dry tiger lily;

then her son and then your man; there you now lie
kept from your father and mother by a layer
of brother and lover and also by

the costumes, wood bronze lead satin silk & wool,
you each wear. Now you, famous for the Saturday
museum-hauls of your New York, ignore the full

shelves of the Costume Museum Out of Mind
you have entered. Once your heels & skirtshapes looked to
Paris; now you notice none of the well defined

custom samples, filed as fashion and history;
beaded dresses, bow ties, hard collars, French chalk,
corsets, false cuffs, union suits, hand embroideries,

and decades of dressed hair, an outgrown show of styles,
some rotted, some stained; yet in your choice place are stored
shapes & modes that amply record our tribal

grasp of the honor of family, the dignity
of ritual, the self of death. There is not much
nourishment in this but I beak it out. Better be

choking down images of the set greywebbed hair
cocoon your skull is wearing and the tumbled nest
of cowlick at your nape, than to grimace and bear

as I bear the packet I found in your drawer, kept
hidden for sixty years but kept: the lissome, fresh,
bright chestnut yard of hair you cut

to enter the nineteen-twenties. Dismay, dismay,
disgusting, it's beautiful, funny, it's yours, mama,
still in tissue paper, boxed, as I throw it away.

CALL

Child like a candelabra at the head
of my bed, wake in me & watch me as
I sleep; maintain your childlife undistracted
where, at the borders of its light, it has
such dulcet limits it becomes the dark.
Maintain against my hungry selfishness
your simple gaze where fear has left no mark.

Today my dead mother to my distress
said on the dreamphone, "Marie, I'll come read
to you," hung up, & in her usual dress
came & stood here. Cold—though I know I need
her true message—I faced her with tenderness
& said, "This isn't right," & she agreed.

Child, watched by your deeper sleep, I may yet say yes.

FRIDAY MARKET

(from Vence, for Mary Denver Candee, 1867-1940)

Under the arch, its ruined walls re-used
as the house-stone of small piles of rooms
(one window each & that spilling flowers)
we enter Old City shadow
on weekly market day.
Tourists, we gossip,
amble, and inspect; handmade candles, sox;
a table strewn with herbs tied in bundles
by grasses, where a child learns her numbers
as her mother makes change; down the street,
leaf-wrapped goat-cheese local as radishes; and
a rosy person selling confections.
I want some. "I make them myself, at my house,"
she says, "of good ingredients."
We buy finger-long beige biscuits, fragrant,
seeded, very tasty, a sackful.
I feel cheerful and grateful.
I eat more than my share.

Days later I wake thinking, "Carroway"—seeds
of such kind sleep as we eat for the sake of descent
to the gone, where I look up safe, years ago.
Mother's mother smiles, shows me a plate of fragrant
carroway cakes, and says, "Take all you want."
I stop crying and do. The seed-bite is telling.
"We have plenty," she says, and I learn
that what she says is true.

MYOPIA MAKES ALL LIGHT SOURCES RADIANT

On the treed slope opposite, vertical
in a close weave of leaves, a giant
woman's face is visible, if
I focus into its shadow-spoken eyes.
. . . it is my face the one
I used to have when in that beauty
all the young own. Its look
is of unripe readiness.

When I put back on my spectacles
it is smiling thoroughly and
is ragged, wrinkled, very old,
its laugh-lines definite,
its softest estimates still
ready to unfold.
It is not symmetrical; one eyebrow
lifts; broad across the forehead
a lock of dark, hair or evergreen,
casts waving shadows.
About the mouth
there is something stricken,
some holm-oak silence facing north.
Winter is coming, giant double-face, old friend.
Winter will replace the persimmon
flagrant at your throat
and the lucky gold fig-tree crown.
To your evergreen mouth only the shape
of your evergreen brow will be

company, as the foliage goes down
flying, worn to the dry fibre,
making its light escape.

IN ABEYANCE

The day of the transit of raptors
happens every September along
the Hudson airlane or updraft;
bird-watchers set a month's mind for it.
No joiner, I'd never joined them
but today from dawn to twelve
high on Hook Mountain I took among friends
with windbreakers cameras binoculars
a watch at a station between fake owls
hoisted on posts facing north & west
to lure the sharp-shins in.
We had the luck to watch
over a hundred (a Cooper's, two marsh, a kettle
of fifty beyond the Tappan Zee); we spent
hours of disembodiment, selves tossed out to vision,
angels in our abeyance, taking gift as title. Tired,
I cased the glasses, ate apples & sandwiches,
lay supine on warm noon rock out of the wind
to magnify sleep with praises of lenses

and woke gasping at shouting, It can't be! It was,
was fluency, inverse above us for hours,
a river swimming with flying a mile deep
among the invisible: all otherness:
          affluence: as twelve thousand
hawks went over, broad-winged
(an eagle among them, osprey also)
the one species mostly; I saw them,
their undulance communal, some

dropping awhile a quarter-mile afloat
then pulsing up again deep.
                    Hawks
splash difference on the visible the
virtual the not-so sky,
displaying the shaping of air
as they plunge up, into out-of-touch, or
as aloft they liquidly
maintain their openness
fully extended to a rest
that rides deeper in the cells
than sleep or than most desire gratified.
There they take their distance
and a stillness to see it in
that I will die knowing nothing inward of.

They know one thing: when.
Days dangle for them, dipping
down & up, then dip less & less
& slow, till left sun & right storm
halt at a balance, & ten thousand
high nests empty as all leap
forward southward from & to
the when of equilibrium.

Together they ebb from us, emigrant,
their perspective on or in
the now of air, transfiguring.

ANALEMMATIC

Shadows matter.
Here in the country of the sun
the shadow of my body measures time.

"Bonnet De Villario struxit."
On a level in Vienne-on-Rhône
his gnomon takes his time.

I as hour-hand and observer of it
put my light-lack on a line
across the stone wheel-track of time.

Outside the squad of the Zodiac, feet joined,
I point my handshape at the spin
of rounders skipping to celestial time

and observe, I am engaged in day-praise:

> Accept, Interrupted Light, this short dark of mine
> personal and visible on account of time.

TAKE TIME, TAKE PLACE

I

There lay Lyonesse, a land now drowned.
There Iseut & Tristan acted, addicted
to love as catapult & drug of destiny.
There, beside themselves, they inflected
the story that shapes us, love misshapen
as fate, its gaunt greed beautiful.
Castle cave & philtre worn to sand & less,
legend washes up in the waters I drink
when, tired of walking free,
I long to abdicate to Lyonesse
in drunken fantasy:
>   Our clean hotel room is sun warmed. As you
>   close with me we sink & sink till we
>   rise under each other borne over
>   in the lifting falling lift
>   of a slow tide quickening.
>   We plunge where joy is, on a leash of air,
>   and re-surface in a double
>   ruffle of water; our joy crests
>   as gasping shaky we draw separate breaths.
>   Sea-water fills our cells
>   while our doubling selves
>   are kept apart by soul & skin.

>   As we dress we glimpse from the windows
>   the low-tide sea snarl, sunstruck above
>   where we may never walk among
>   the shadowshapes of fatal urgency,

for it is sunken, sunken,
that honeysuckle land,
its fort rings skyless, nothing left
but seven stones standing and they
under water at high tide.
It is lost, the desirable paradise
     where love greedy as dreams is fatal & excused,
lost, and the road to it
lost, and its amorous acts
pickled in brine.

Sleep take it. Awake I like a drier wine.

Though under the wish to sluice off
wounds and the memory of wounds
I dream I dive hand in hand
with both Iseuts, wordlessly
learning to live breathless their doomed way,
in fact even in that dark I feel a stricter lift
of longing for times of choice in the light of day

where I'd say many things to you but never
     lie and say, "I couldn't help myself";

where I'd have good dreams clear of doom & mystery
     and learn in from out, responsible as ecstasy;
where I might take time, take place, mind memory.

2

Time & travel change my mind.
Their implicit courses
make choosing more complex;
I lose the single scope

small choice protects.
All choices are losses—except
for true remembrance which sharpens
blunt intentions into acts,
or for false fantasy
which makes bandages of torn-up facts
to stem the haemorrhage of memory.

The landscape I have left behind
waits for me.
In fantasy, I need not remember it:
If I want, it is weather-free,
its mental climate generous;
I can call in, recklessly,
two moons or suns, calm or storm,
and any company.
Those I'd invite wd come peaceably,
the strong, the witty, but done with dispute—
Launcelot, Elizabeth, Finn,
Dilly Dedalus no longer mute
wd join my old friends, first love, lost kin
all looking as I'd wish they'd be,
at ease as hero & heroine.

Effortlessly helpful
like a southern slope, the people
at timeless picnics can praise a sky
clear without their hope;
they can agree about the food, real cream,
trees of sunwarm fruit, good bread.
They are the people I need
as much as solitude;
they'd all smile, according to this scheme,
not disliking me, not dead,
lost, or dischronous, but well met
and interviewed.

These haunts of wish are falsely true.

Real dream-work builds a windbreak
for retrieval & repair.
But I abuse it when I sleep awake,
to hide from grief I will not bear,
in its shadow-acclimated air.
It is rich, such nowhere.

3

Fantasies dampen the pang of cherishing
goods and chances lost or left behind.
I do no work; they can bring back everything
in waves of picture-music, filmy, soft-spined:
melons can bulge above thin greens of spring
as snowmelt swamps the brookbank to scare
big August moths while yes the applerind
reddens in flowering orchards, near where
live & dead share breakfast and at last find
intimate approval easy, in air
which such reverie, obliterating
absence, swindles to vision I can bear
since nothing is asked of me. Day dreaming
reforms loss till it is neither here nor there.

Loss reformed till it is neither here nor there
is double loss. Then let the absent shout
and shake pain's shameful scent on the air—
that will shock the old fact-faces out:
dank spring panic, my fate-embracing stare,
your rage, mine. Let the early dead speak again,
this time to untell the lies death left in doubt;
let their harsh loss start my resurrection
in the plural truth they were and are about.

Though the dead have sealed their eyes and arguments
and seasons irk or please us unaware,
marked in the far hawk and the daily wren
the great co-ordinates, perfectly fair,
might haul this place now up through that place then.

This place now—if hauled through that place then
whose salt inner seas lighten my real weight—
beaches my self in my shape, dries my skin,
& grounds me where I can stand to integrate
the crazy hot-cold climates I have chosen
or been chosen by. Bodies met in dream
that I once by drift-fire took to my embrace
confront me as stroke for stroke I redeem
that flesh with this. Time interpenetrates
the memory: match-flare, full blaze, fading gleam,
morning ash. Waking I see as they were then
the lost, towering, remote, but true, their beam
sentinel. I hear old names true-spoken
in the chuckle of the channeled inner stream.

Down the chuckle of the channeled inner stream
I stare for signs, imagining replies,
& endure in echo the spent grunts & screams,
the true relics of my victims & allies.
I squat & study what they meant to mean
and fail but listen: I've stopped saying yes
to the doom of being what I must despise;
doom is not self but a game, a guess,
a child's costume—and a deadly disguise
I can just get rid of like an ugly dress.
The hard sun of memory, in wisps of steam,
lifts off the make-up, the splotches of distress,
dries up the marsh-wraith veil of false esteem,
and sets off alarm-clocks sharp as happiness.

They set me off, alarmed at happiness,
to join birds in their sanctuary. A tern flies
tilting to its turns with acute finesse.
I watch it mediate marsh & beach, skies
and ocean, balancing stress & stress,
airlift & gravity, with unminded ease.
Its caught fish flashes, swallowed on the rise.
Its high speed fueled by its discoveries,
it pipe-threads upward as its black beak dries.
Its life embraces its necessities;
this federal parkland is its wilderness.
Such grace. It names the saving world I might seize
but am too locked in time to see: unless
we are what our imagination frees.

To become what my imagination frees
my road turns linear. Summer gardens die
a while, above the ground's certain mysteries;
winter shines & deepens like a sleep; but I
leave Eden joyfully; all cyclic repose
dims the human joy I can't afford to lose,
the causeless joy that hears joy as a reply,
and turns my hand to what's left of my true
experiment in the forward of surprise.
Joy's like luck, imagine that! I can't
lose or win it, mean or wild, off or on my knees.
Joy speaks out And in. The time-line joy may use
is broken and brightens not as I please
but any instant. Its innocence accrues.

On the instant, its innocence accrues
across the cityscape, real and immense.
Here bird and I are each other's news
alighting centered in the present tense.
Inside out I identify bird clues

framed in sun by my binocular guess;
here its lift of head & tail are evidence
its flash of song confirms; here is steadfastness
in single names for thick experience.
"Wren," I say. "Hawk." "Tern." "Luck." "Love." Wingless
and winged we startle then settle, each a view,
alert & modest in our different dress.
I hear unearned joy pay my human dues
and take this passage for my new address.

Climbing the steps, awake, I wake to sense
how dream-tides shape all shores, their forward press
rich in suspended dissolute continents;
and deep under the seas' collapsing caress
are the porches and bridals of Lyonesse.

From *The Bird Catcher*, 1998

"I'VE BEEN AROUND: IT GETS ME NOWHERE"

"Cuncta fui; conducit nihil."

V. AURELIUS

I am the woman always too young to be
holding the diamond the baby exulting.

I am the worker afraid of the rules & the boss; my
salary heats the house where I feed many children.

I am packing my bags for coming & going
& going much further than ever before.

> Though elsewhere gets me nowhere
> place is not a problem.
> Feet keep me going,
> the impressive exporters
> of what place is about. Maps—
> gold on parchment or printed
> Mobil travel ads—lay it all out.

> But over every place, time goes
> remote, a cloud-cover question.
> You, in love with your castle, your jet,
> your well-invested dollars
> and I with my moving
> dictionaries & binoculars
> are both almost out of it,
> too far gone to find a bin
> with stores of more time in.
> A decade, a week, a second, then
> time shrugs and shudders out of touch
> into a perfect fit,
> and that's it.

I am the dog I let out in the morning
wagging & panting at the open door.

I am the foresworn child in the swing
arching & pumping, practicing, "More, more!"

I'm the crossword puzzle time & place
bound at the end by their loose embrace.

OLD MAMA SATURDAY

("Saturday's child must work for a living")

"I'm moving from Grief Street.
Taxes are high here
though the mortgage's cheap.

The house is well built.
With stuff to protect, that
mattered to me,
the security.

These things that I mind,
you know, aren't mine.
I mind minding them.
They weigh on my mind.

I don't mind them well.
I haven't got the knack
of kindly minding.
I say Take them back
but you never do.

When I throw them out
it may frighten you
and maybe me too.

     Maybe
it will empty me
too emptily

and keep me here

asleep, at sea
under the guilt quilt,
under the you tree."

NORTHAMPTON STYLE

Evening falls. Someone's playing a dulcimer
Northampton-style, on the porch out back.
Its voice touches and parts the air of summer,

as if it swam to time us down a river
where we dive and leave a single track
as evening falls. Someone's playing a dulcimer

that lets us wash our mix of dreams together.
Delicate, tacit, we engage in our act;
its voice touches and parts the air of summer.

When we disentangle you are not with her
I am not with him. Redress calls for tact.
Evening falls. Someone's playing a dulcimer

still. A small breeze rises and the leaves stir
as uneasy as we, while the woods go black;
its voice touches and parts the air of summer

and lets darkness enter us, our strings go slack
though the player keeps up his plangent attack.
Evening falls. Someone's playing a dulcimer;
its voice touches and parts the air of summer.

THE TITLE'S LAST

Here's the best joke, though its flavor is salt:
the bad company I've kept, the bad risks I've run
have left me standing (a figure of fun
but) one at whose shadow some strangers halt.

I've been pole when some asked, so they could vault
supported, high as they like, letting me drop
intact, and roll safe to a grassy stop.
We've gone our ways with pleasure and without fault,
they to the next race, I to the next use
poles are put to by the great competitors.

Self-schooled I've been fish, ocean floors
wrinkling my shadow, flashing free, loose,
in my long survival of all I've done—
for sharks that bite me eat death by poison,
le requin qui me mord s'empoisonne.

ONE IS ONE

Heart, you bully, you punk, I'm wrecked, I'm shocked
stiff. You? you still try to rule the world—though
I've got you: identified, starving, locked
in a cage you will not leave alive, no
matter how you hate it, pound its walls,
& thrill its corridors with messages.

Brute. Spy. I trusted you. Now you reel & brawl
in your cell but I'm deaf to your rages,
your greed to go solo, your eloquent
threats of worse things you (knowing me) could do.
You scare me, bragging you're a double agent

since jailers are prisoners' prisoners too.
Think! Reform! Make us one. Join the rest of us,
and joy may come, and make its test of us.

POURRITURE NOBLE

a moral tale, for Sauternes, the fungus cenaria, *and the wild old*

Never prophesy.
You can't. So don't try.
Lust, pride, and lethargy
may cause us misery
or bliss.
The meanest mistake
has a point to make.
Hear this—
what his vintner d'Eyquem said
once the lord d'Eyquem was dead:
    "The wine that year promised bad or none.
    He'd let it go too late.
    Rot had crawled through all the vines,
    greasy scum on every cluster
    dangling at the crotches of the leaves.
    Should have been long picked
    but he'd said, 'No. Wait for me,'
    off to wait on a new woman,
    grapes on the verge of ripe
    when he left. Coupling kept him
    till rot wrapped the grapes like lace
    & by the time she'd kicked him out
    the sun had got them, they hung
    shriveled in the blast.

    Well, he rode home cocky
    & bullied the grapes into the vats
    rot & all, spoiled grapes, too old,
    too soon squeezed dry.

The wine makes.
The wine makes thick, gold-colored,
& pours like honey.
We try it. Fantastic!
not like honey, punchy,
you've never drunk anything like it—
refreshing, in a rush
over a heat that slows your throat—
wanting to keep that flavor
stuck to the edge of your tongue
where your taste is, keep it
like the best bouquet you can remember
of sundown summer & someone coming
to you smiling. The taste has odor
like a new country, so fine
at first you can't take it in
it's so strange. It's beautiful
& believe me you love to go slow."

moral:

Age is not
all dry rot.
It's never too late.
Sweet is your real estate.

FOR MY OLD SELF, AT NOTRE-DAME

fluctuat nec mergitur

The dark madonna cut from a knot of wood
has robes whose folds make waves against the grain
and a touching face—noble in side view,
impish or childish seen head-on from above.
The wood has the rich stain of tannin, raised
to all-color lustre by the steep of time.

The mouths of her shadows are pursed by time
to suck sun-lit memories from the wood.
Freezing damp and candle-smut have raised
her eyebrows into wings flung up by the grain,
caught in the light of bulbs plugged high above.
She stands alert, as if hailed, with beasts in view.

Outside on the jeweled river-ship, I view
a girl's back, walking off. Oh. Just in time
I shut up. She'd never hear me shout above
the tour-guides and ski-skate kids. How I would
have liked to see her face again, the grain
of beauty on her forehead, her chin raised

startled; her Who are you? wild, a question raised
by seeing me, an old woman, in plain view.
Time is a tree in me; in her it's a grain
ready to plant. I go back in, taking my time
leafy among stone trunks that soar in stone woods
where incense drifts, misty, lit pink from above.

She's headed for her hotel room then above
Cluny's garden. She'll sit there then, feet raised,
notebook on her knees, to write. Maybe she would
have heard, turned, known us both in a larger view
and caught my age in the freshness of its time.
She dreads clocks, she says. Such dry rot warps the grain.

They still say mass here. Wine and wheat-grain
digest to flesh in words that float above
six kneeling women, a man dressed outside time,
and the dark madonna, her baby raised
dangerously high to pull in our view.
Magic dame, cut knot, your ancient wood

would reach back to teach her if it could. Spring rain.
Through it I call to thank her, loud above
the joy she raised me for, this softfall. Sweet time.

THE BORDER

(Annuals & Perennials, Mixed)

She kneels to the yellow short flowers
velvety, feathery, lit. Pansies
are for thoughts, she knows,
and, Pick lots but pick them
in the morning so they last.

The can of salted water is for slugs.
It kills them dead, quietly.
She finds one bigger than her thumb.
She looks away to drop it in but
hears it drop. She's taller this year;
standing she can gaze downward into
the iris Queen Maud a white crown
on the stem that presents it
above the crowded pansy border.

Next Saturday at Dorothea's wedding
she'll be the flower girl
with a crown of baby's breath clipped
to her slippery dutch-bob hair.

She must remember / she'd better practice
Left Foot First, this week,
every time she walks.
Grandma says, It's all right, dear,
all eyes will be on the bride.

The earliest tree peony is out,
alba, it smells like roses among
the garden's almost-summer smell.

She sits on the steps; they're hot
not too hot. She picks up her blue pipe.
Beside her the bowl
holds water gluey with soap
& drops of grandma's glycerine.
The pipe-cup breaks its disk of light.

Trying to be even & be slow
she bites on the pipe-stem.
Her breath steadies;
she blows out a bubble,
another, the two
float over the pansies
into the bridal-wreath bush
and disappear.

Getting married is like that.
Getting married is not like that.

SEPARATE, IN THE SWIM

(Temara Plage, Morocco)

Oiled and drowsy, idling in a sling
of turquoise cotton, you take the sun.

I stow my rings, cash, shirt, & frayed
cords of connection under your chair.

I cross bands of hot sand then damp cool,
to the waves rustling up
broken by the aim of wave, the idea
that picks up the water
and throws it at the shore.

Invading the invading sea, leaning to it
arms at an angle, I wade in slowly,
weight forward, leading with my knees,
soft-jumping in answer to wave-swell.

Wet to the hips I dive under
and swim turning in to pleasure.
The sea surges inshore. I surge out.

The seas alter me and alter after me,
allowing me a horizontal stride.
Armstrokes & legstrokes echo in my cells
heating the circuit of blood.

Each stroke starts a far drumming
clumping the kelp, helping
shells and rubbish decay into sand.
I press out a pulse (it will

throb back as another pulse) along
the sea-floor and the furthest beaches.
In this stretch of the Atlantic
the whole Atlantic operates.

As I ride, its broad cast evokes
my tiny unity, a pod, a person.

Thanks to the closure of skin
I'm forking the tune I'm part of
though my part is played moving
on a different instrument.
I hear the converse of wave-work
fluid in counterpoint, the current
unrupturing. I push: the Atlantic
resists so that I can push myself

toward a music which on this scale
is balance, balancing buoyancies,
able to condense me back out with it
having carried my will
forward a while before
it carries me to shore.

You have slept.
You have taken the sun.
I towel myself dry

THE STORY AFTER THE STORY

In bubbles to the elbow, on my knees,
I am washing children. You are laughing,
pleased to observe me at my mysteries.

Antoine & Will giggle as I sluice their backs.
My knees soaked by local tidal splashes
creak as I stand and towel two relaxed

bed-ready boys. I crib them, warm in their
soft shirts, & sit to eat a bruised sweet apple
as I nurse Chris and float on mild air

a story for everyone; Monique & Denis
settle on child-chairs; we are a tangle,
bitch and pups, in the oldest comity.

You like that less, leave us for the kitchen
to finish the fruit and cheese. The ample
story falls short on me. My mind itches.

Sighing & smiling Antoine drops to sleep.
Will lies awake, only his eyes active.
Monique trusts the story somehow to keep

mapping new ways home through more & more world.
Chris drowses. Will's eyelids lift up, lapse back.
Denis' fists lie in his lap, loosely curled.

I am willing them one by one to sleep.
The story wanders in its adjectives.
Chris' mouth clamps down, lets go, breathes deep.

Humming & murmuring I bed them all.
Monique tells a soft story, managing
me into mind with her as she too falls.

I rise in joy, ready, the child-work done.
I find you have gone out. A radical
of loss cancels what we might have become.

ROUNDSTONE COVE

The wind rises. The sea snarls in the fog
far from the attentive beaches of childhood—
no picnic, no striped chairs, no sand, no sun.

Here even by day cliffs obstruct the sun;
moonlight miles out mocks this abyss of fog.
I walk big-bellied, lost in motherhood,

hunched in a shell of coat, a blindered hood.
Alone a long time, I remember sun—
poor magic effort to undo the fog.

Fog hoods me. But the hood of fog is sun.

READING A LARGE SERVING DISH

(Greek, ca. 400 B.C., Art Institute of Chicago)

Persephone white-faced
carries her vegetal cross
on a stalk perpendicular
over her shoulder as she heads
up & out for home
& mother, her brilliant mother.

Closing, Hell's house lies behind her
(and, of course, opening, before).

Four creamy horses
implacably processional
are hauling her chariot
—red-orange on black ceramic—
toward her spring turn of sky.
They head for the edge
of the dish of plenty that honors
her style of exchange (exile for exile)
and her game of rounders (no winners, no losers)
her poverty her plenty.

> The dish itself is Demosthenes' age.
> Its suave lines issue its invitation,
> open-ended, a strange attractor.
>
> It tells you it will
> if you eat from it teach
> your deepening night to brighten

at the depth where no gesture
is straightforward or false,
and you do not need to expect
you can rise beyond suffering.

ANALYSIS

Analysis prefers a mountain lake
without tributaries to account for.
It can't stand random splashing, can't just take
its clothes off and jump in. Its designs score
by degrees: first it looks, till it seizes
a sense of the whole; then it stares some more,
till the rippling surface stills & freezes.
Its bubbles flatten hard and rim the shore.

And now analysis cuts the ice to bits,
tens or thousands, each a telling device
flashing "lake" in part-song, true in how it fits
the cutter's visionary set for ice.

Patterns lapse in a bliss of signal mist
which concludes in the swim of the analyst.

TWO QUESTIONS

FOR E. COLEMAN, L. FERLINGHETTI, E. FONTINELL, G. MALLY,
D. YEZZO, ALL MEN OF GOOD WILL AND SOMETIME ARMED FORCES

I

Dropped
brilliant
in such windrush he
can't scream
he's moving too
fast in the pitchblack
falling his
parachute hot buckles & charred string

he is on fire he hits salt
water, goes out   as he
goes under. It chokes with
him in his throat,
that shout.

Fire, the flare human, the
body of burning plunging,
shot star sea-quenched:
. . . fifty years on fire in my mind.

Second hand. Dreamed, dreamed,
a silence of scream, heat
into cold, extinguishing.
Waked by, wept for, guessed at,
an ignorant dream, dreaming those
who flew to kill again toward gunfire
flew killed flew killed flew   But he
burned, that boy, my age, Lt. Little,

prayed for in my parish monthly thirty years
till his mother died; who else would remember?
His lovers at then twenty-one
have long loved others. Only those
who made him up out of anguish
ignorant among war news remember
what the order of murder made.

2

Wasp & osprey flee our ring of discord
but now & then—as if some beast were fat
& we winter-struck with hunger—
we close in on it flourishing weaponry
and war makes meat of some.

In their poor young butchers
otherwise virtuous   it taints memory
with ownerless bitterness.

Our catch-basin cities swirl with blood
until—some larder stocked—we stop
come home   wash up   and restore
peace as if there were no war.

If slaughter always alters our memory
if brutal mistakes are fatal so far
& if I—no Amazon, no Lysistrata—agree
no life is free of brute fatality

what is a safe childhood for?

of what is war the history?

PRE-TEXT

FOR DOUGLAS, AT ONE

Archaic, his gestures
hieratic, just like Caesar or Sappho
or Mary's Jesus or Ann's Mary or Jane
Austen once, or me or your mother's you

the sudden baby surges to his feet
and sways, head forward, chin high,
arms akimbo, hands dangling idle,
elbows up, as if winged.

The features of his face stand out
amazed, all eyes as his aped posture
sustains him aloft
               a step a step a rush
and he walks,

Young Anyone, his lifted point of view
far beyond the calendar.

What time is it? Firm in time
he is out of date—

like a cellarer for altar wines
tasting many summers in one glass,

or like a grandmother
in whose womb her
granddaughter once
slept in egg inside
grandma's unborn daughter's
folded ovaries.

EXPLORERS CRY OUT UNHEARD

What I have in mind is the last wilderness.

I sweat to learn its heights of sun, scrub, ants,
its gashes full of shadows and odd plants,
as inch by inch it yields to my hard press.

And the way behind me changes as I advance.
If interdependence shapes the biomass,
though I plot my next step by pure chance
I can't go wrong. Even willful deviance
connects me to all the rest. The changing past
includes and can't excerpt me. Memory grants
just the nothing it knows, & my distress
drives me toward the imagined truths I stalk,
those savages. Warned by their haunting talk,
their gestures, I guess they mean no. Or yes.

WINTER

I don't know what to say to you, neighbor,
as you shovel snow from your part of our street
neat in your Greek black. I've waited for
chance to find words; now, by chance, we meet.

We took our boys to the same kindergarten,
thirteen years ago when our husbands went.
Both boys hated school, dropped out feral, dropped in
to separate troubles. You shift snow fast, back bent,
but your boy killed himself, six days dead.

My boy washed your wall when the police were done.
He says, "We weren't friends?" and shakes his head,
"I told him it was great he had that gun,"
and shakes. I shake, close to you, close to you.
You have a path to clear, and so you do.

OCEANS

FOR WILLIAM COOK, DROWNED IN MAINE, AND
FOR ROY HUSS, LOST IN INDONESIA

Death is breath-taking. We all die young,
our lives defined by failure of the heart,
our fire drowned in failure of the lungs.
Still planning on pouring the best ripe part
of wines our need or grasp has sucked or wrung
from fruit & sun, we're stopped before we start.
Taste like talk fades from the stiffening tongue.

In reach of what we've wanted, our hope is strung
toward closing chords of accomplishment; we
grip ourselves.
    Cut off we go stunned, raw
as a land-child brought out to see only
ocean all the way to sky. Shut in awe
we wrap our secret in us as we die
unsaid, the deaf objects of good-by.

EVEN

I

Were there cliffs cupping Eden?
I think it so   just high enough
for the travel of shadows & echoes

Vegetal animal
Eden was nothing
Adam was nothing

> *Animal   vegetal*
> *he is on stage a while*
> *before he speaks*
>
> *From wing to wing*
> *air lifts and rustles*
> *The light is general*
> *a wonderful consonance*

Adam wakes present
in the present tense
to his present Eve

Eve comes to

Adam was nothing
not even lonely   till
Eve came to
          listening

In Eve's eyes
Adam is faced

Each is the only equal
They stand definite
the same in their luminous skins
their faces regarded the same

        Adam is / Eve is
        nothing   much yet but
        by their same difference
        Eden is seen to be everywhere
        What they see is Eden

                        Being

Eve came to invent us
        invent audience
taking in hearing
she came to hear him:
        sponsa
        respondens

        the birth of responsible life

He would hear her
she would be there to hear

        With trials of consonants
        labials gutturals stops
                out of breath
        Adam begins: Br. Sh. Th. Kr.

    The names stick.
    The air waits. Eden
    fades   the beasts
    stop short   the river
    threatens to harden.
        Adam's skull
    stammers & hurts

Eve opens her ears

She is   listening

On the waves the whorls embraced
Adam came   to her mind
as the sound of Adam

Her throat aches

a great longing
"Ah," she replied

"ah"

o Eve is out in the open
a toss-up of vowels & verbs

Her diverted breath informed her

loosening vision & interludes
fluency   silence
a diverse civility

Aren't they something
Both are the only equal
and the speaking listener

Eden's creatures, eased, began flexing
out of their names their spines & joints
crackled & shone   acting in syntax
answering   her answering
flowering vines
hung fruited with stories

Through each other
microscope telescope
they look at the garden
Landscape enlarges them

    The oxen lift their knees
    the baboon flaunts its pink
    the various frogs
    touch the high pitch & low
    of audible sound Their range
    arranges them articulate

Syllables act on the two
who hearing say Syllable
—action syntaction
how touching what tact
Invented by listening
sound invents sentences.

The breeze drags fragrance through consensual intervals of air.

Confirmed by cliffs, their usual gaze
looked not down but across
neither upwards but on the level
at Eden each other.
Journeys never occurred to them
even at evening
when the only Other often arrived
and they breathed in.

    Together they breathe
    that Other breath.

      They breathe that in & out
      they keep on breathing.

2

In a sift of ash in Wales,
at the bottom of a pit sunk
in the crucial chamber of a passage grave,
its stones cut & laid up dry
5,000 years ago, about, diggers found
and anatomists identified a small
bone of the inner ear. It is that of a girl
8 to 10 years old, in perfect condition.

Lost is found. Salvation.
I happened to hear of it.

If I can hear this
what may I not hear

Sight's the electric hunger, though sensual Blake
says hearing's the most intimate appetite.

Bird what do you praise Praise it
again among the juniper plumes
& silvered-blue juniper berrybeads

Your birdpraise rivers the juniper air
until I admit the incision of listening,
and self rising easily up off the river
evaporates altered into its liberty

3

Sundown, & under the afterglow
woods and fields fall still.
Hidden, the daycreatures drowse.

Nightcreatures step soft; rabbits go cautious
& the hunt is up for the unwary in-between.

Under the trees fireflies exclaim.
After dinner city people on vacation
hold hands, having been promised the moon
which is rising up a dark-collecting sky.
It is June, trees hold still, the breeze
holds its breath. I stroll out into the dim field
open to great horned owls, too big to fear them.

My mother & father are walking out
hand in hand in my mind of summer
into the shadowed meadow
crowded with flickering lights
in the Poconos in nineteen-nineteen
under their honeymoon.

He calls them lightning bugs, she laughs & says
Fireflies though the hotel receptionist
said there were glow-worms, how funny.

They do not plan to remember it all their lives
but they do. Haunted by silence, they do.
It wasn't easily talked of. All I know is,
neither ever saw again
such shining flying in every direction,
acres of low-lying air where wild sparks
pulsed silent in the dark. Until they died,
it would flare up in them at times.

He turned the talk to the lightning of storms,
listening to her fear & attraction; always
he answered around her to keep her if he could
from hurting, with her wit where he was tender,

or with slow tears if his wit spoke.
It got better after twenty years or so.
They found themselves
each in the other's power & lost dread.
He would or she would take turns
managing to dredge up hope
in rummaging just for luck
for heaven in the marriage
that was their Lost & Found.

    Write lost as cost;
    spell fond, spell fund, spell found;
    spell band, spell bond, spell-bound.

And as well, if you will,
spell promise, premise;
    ratified,
    gratified.

4

After judgment & the wet sacrament of slaughter,

greener than Eden, a shock of bliss to see
just past the stew & suck of reeking waters,
the earth ate sunshine under the olive trees.

Noah, his wife, their sons, their daughters
rushed to lower the gangplank. Awkward, long doubled,
unboxed & jostling, the passengers suddenly free
hustled uncoupling ashore to uncouple, suddenly free.

A Note About the Author

Marie Ponsot's first book of poems was *True Minds* (1956); later books are *Admit Impediment* (1981) and *The Green Dark* (1988). She is a native New Yorker who has enjoyed teaching at Queens College, Beijing United University, the Poetry Center of the YMHA, New York University, and Columbia University. Among her awards are an NEA Creative Writing grant, the Delmore Schwartz Memorial Prize, and the Shaughnessy Medal of the Modern Language Association. Ponsot's most recent collection, *The Bird Catcher*, won the National Book Critics Circle Award for Poetry in 1998.

A Note on the Type

This book was set in Adobe Garamond. Designed for the Adobe Corporation by Robert Slimbach, the fonts are based on types first cut by Claude Garamond (c. 1480–1561). Garamond was a pupil of Geoffroy Tory and is believed to have followed the Venetian models, although he introduced a number of important differences, and it is to him that we owe the letter we now know as "old style." He gave to his letters a certain elegance and feeling of movement that won their creator an immediate reputation and the patronage of Francis I of France.

Composed by Creative Graphics,
Allentown, Pennsylvania
Printed and bound by Berryville Graphics,
Berryville, Virginia
Designed by Anthea Lingeman